Missionary Stories on Safari

Missionary Stories
on Safari

Lorna Eglin

CF4•K

10 9 8 7 6 5 4 3 2 1
© Copyright 2009 Lorna Eglin
Christian Focus Publications
ISBN: 978-1-84550-505-9
Published by Christian Focus Publications,
Geanies House, Fearn, Tain, Ross-shire,
IV20 1TW, Scotland, U.K.
www.christianfocus.com
email:info@christianfocus.com

Cover design by Daniel van Straaten
Illustrations by Fred Apps
Printed and bound by Norhaven, Denmark

This book is dedicated to Betty Allcock

who enjoyed these Safaris with me.

Also, to the faithful supporters who,

in Jesus' name, have enabed us to go on many safaris,

by their generous giving over the forty-five years covered by

these stories, for the about fifteen vehicles we have worn out

in God's service.

Contents

What is a Safari?

When tourists thinks of a safari they think of luxury, ease, exotic food and game watching. They might rough it a little in a tent but there would be a grass roof over it to keep it cool, with mosquito protection and a tiled bathroom with water on tap, and all mod-cons provided.

However, when we missionaries write about going "on safari," we mean something very different! We mean battling with deep dust or bogging-down mud, on unbelievably bad roads. It's not a luxury holiday but basic living, eating local food and having adventures at every turn. So in this book we invite you to go on safari with us to see what a Kenyan safari, not a tourist one, really is.

The word "safari" is the Kiswahili word for "journey" which can be catching a bus to the next town or walking ten miles to visit your grandmother. These days a safari may be made by plane, train, boat or even bicycle. The rural Kenyans are great walkers – taking a fifteen-mile walk to church on Sunday in their stride. All these are "safaris" and when the traveller arrives he is greeted with, 'Habari ya safari?' – How was your journey?

Our "safaris" were made in a variety of vehicles over the years. We became very fond of most of our four-wheeled friends. They were our very necessary fellow-workers, usually reliable, and doing what was required of them.

These safaris often turned into adventures - engine failure fifty miles from the nearest mechanic, or the third puncture when we had only two spare wheels. But the best adventures happened when we arrived at our destination. Instead of hunting animals missionaries hunt people, people who have not heard of Jesus. They go to make friends, to chat and to bring the message of God to their new friends.

So let's go on safari together, and share our adventures with you!

My First Real Safari

'You have failed!' the traffic policeman snapped at me, not unexpectedly, as I had reversed into the wall at the end of my driver's test. 'Come back next week. Spend those days gaining some skill in reversing!'

I wanted to have a driver's licence in hand when I went to work in Kenya. I was soon to board the ship to set off on my missionary career. I had a vague idea that being able to drive might be a useful asset in my new, unknown life.

'Oh! Please sir,' I wailed. 'I am leaving the country in three days' time. Give me another chance!' The policeman smiled.

'Sure, come back this afternoon at two o'clock. Seeing you are leaving the country, you are no threat to any of our citizens. But please try not to damage any more walls!'

I spent the hours till two o'clock practising and went home triumphantly clutching a driver's licence. All walls had been left intact! I took the licence with me to Kenya, but not having my own car, I had no chance of practice, so the little skill I had got rusty.

Then came the wonderful day when a fellow missionary and I bought a strong, 4x4 pick-up. We each wrote out a cheque for our share and I climbed up nervously into the driver's seat. Everything seemed huge and unfamiliar, but I fiddled with the gear lever and turned on the engine. The car leapt forward! My fumbling with the gear lever had not found neutral! I climbed down even more nervously.

'Your car has very good advice written on the front,' a laughing bystander remarked to me. Puzzled, I walked to the front to look. "DODGE BROTHERS", the logo of the manufacturers, was displayed clearly for all to see. This was the way my long driving career started. But on that day I persuaded the other missionary to do the driving.

Back home we practised on short trips and soon felt ready for a real safari. Down in the hot valley below us there were very few Christians. We arranged with two others to join us along the way – a missionary who was a nurse, and a Kenyan evangelist who spoke the language of the people we were going to. The other missionary and I were learning it, but were not yet very fluent.

On the great day we piled the back of the car with camp-cots, bedding, pots and pans, eating utensils, some food and a few clothes, a variety of medicines and all that would be needed in setting up a makeshift clinic down in the valley.

We were excited and fearful – a good feeling for an unknown adventure. I bravely took the wheel first. We started off through forest, so dense that the road seldom dried out. After ten miles we dropped, with a series of frightening hairpin bends, down to the valley where we crossed a short bridge made from a few planks of wood nailed together. It was well reinforced but with no sides to stop us toppling into the river. We nervously edged our way over.

After a few more miles we met up with the others who were joining our safari. As we loaded their luggage into the back of the pickup the missionary bemoaned the fact that she had forgotten her bag of clothes. We assured her that clothes didn't matter at all – she could share ours. It was far more important that she'd remembered to bring food. When we'd checked that she had, we drove on. The young Kenyan evangelist with her said very little but kept smiling widely at whatever was happening.

We turned off the main road onto a track winding its way down the valley. The land was flat and dry. There were no people, no herds, no flocks. We wondered why we had come! Back home we had been praying for the people of the valley, that they would hear the good news of God's love. But our young "Smiler" assured us that there were many people ahead.

'It would be good to stop a few miles further on,' he suggested. 'There is a little house that government officials use to sleep in when they come down this valley.' We cheered up as we pictured comfort and even perhaps a bit of luxury! The following day would be busy once we'd found the people. The other two ladies were both nurses and planned to set up an impromptu clinic. This would be a good way to contact the people so that then they might be willing to listen to our message from God.

We travelled on, but our visions of luxury, or even comfort, died quickly the moment we spotted the house we were aiming for. It was a small mud-walled building with a grass roof. Most of the mud had cracked and fallen off and much of the grass had been blown away. The door and windows were just open, empty spaces.

While we unpacked camp-cots, sleeping bags and food for supper, Smiler quickly disappeared, found some dry twigs, lit a fire and had a kettle of water nearly on the boil. The tea he made was refreshing but we were still hot, dusty and sweaty and longed for a wash. Smiler went off to look for more sticks for our supper fire and returned with a bigger smile.

'I have found a small muddy dam just over that rise. You could go and wash there, while I peel the potatoes for supper.' Happily we went to the dam and found mostly mud, but on one side there was a little water and flat rocks we could stand on to wash. Two of us managed successfully. But our third lady slipped off a rock and fell, splash, into the muddy water!

'I have nothing to change into,' she wailed. We quickly promised her some clothes from our meagre stock. Much later, when we had eaten a good supper, we prayed, then planned the next day with its activities. Smiler slept in the car, and we got ready for bed. I changed into my pyjamas and carefully draped my clothes, piece by piece, across the sill of the empty window. My clothes were not too dirty, so, as the party was now rather short of clothes, I planned to wear the same ones the next day.

I got up early the next day but as I picked up my clothes from the window sill there was some resistance and a tearing sound. I looked closer and saw hundreds of white insects scuttling away into their mud tunnels. Termites had destroyed my precious clothes completely! As I dressed in my only change of clean clothes I discussed our predicament with the other missionaries. None of us now had any spare clean clothes left!

We breakfasted, packed up and within five miles found the hordes of people we had hoped for. There were houses, enclosures for the cattle and goats, and lots of activity. Children quickly gathered round the car gawking at the strange-looking people inside.

Soon three important-looking men sauntered over and we got out to greet them and explain ourselves. They were very glad for their people to receive free medical treatment. Soon our folding table and chairs were set up in the shade of a scrawny tree and "sipitali" (hospital) was underway. Smiler helped the nurses and interpreted for everyone.

I felt rather useless, but I had brought a tough wooden record player with stories recorded in the local language. I sat under another tree and soon had a crowd of children listening, wondering how a man could get inside that little box!

When the clinic was over, the people gathered willingly to hear what we had to say. The missionaries tried to give a short message, but Smiler had to explain what we had meant to say. He then added his own clear message of God's love for us. We told them of Jesus. They listened quietly, but with dull looks on their faces.

'Have you ever heard these words before?' I asked some women. They looked at me blankly and said that all this was new to them. I tried a group of men.

'Fathers,' I asked politely, 'These words we have brought today – have you heard them before?' They shook their heads, 'No, we have never heard that God has a Son!' Another man spoke up. 'I heard something about God having a Son when I was up the hills at the hospital. But I was very sick. I didn't remember his name.' I asked many people, 'Have you heard about Jesus, God's Son, before today?' But, to nearly all, the name Jesus, or the idea of God having a Son, was completely unknown.

Suddenly a scene of my schooldays came back to me. I was at a Girls Camp. It was Sunday morning and we were sitting on the ground, in the shade. It was church time and a visiting missionary was to give us the sermon. She caught my attention because I noticed she was holding a big bag of sweets in her hand as she came forward - it was going to be an interesting sermon!

'Would you like a sweet?' she asked. She had first arranged us into groups and then she asked this question of the one nearest me. Of course they each took a sweet gladly.

'Eat them,' she encouraged. They obeyed with a bit of a giggle.

'Did you enjoy the sweet? Have another,' she said handing them round again. And again! We started murmuring and looking at each other.

'Give us some too!' one brave girl called out. The missionary tossed one in her direction but kept giving her chosen group another, and yet another sweet, until we were in an uproar!

'That's not fair!' we called out, catching on to what she was doing. 'Give sweets to all of us! Why should the one group have them all?' Then she stopped and turned to us.

'That is why I am a missionary,' she explained with great feeling. 'It is not right that some people are told about Jesus over and over again, while others are completely left out. All people need to hear the sweet message of God's love.' She went on to tell us of her missionary work and that many people are still left out, not knowing about Jesus.

I was in my last year in high school and, as I loved Jesus and wanted to serve Him, I had been praying about what God wanted me to do with my life. At that moment God spoke clearly to me, into my heart.

'This is what you are to do. Take the message of my love to people who have never heard of Jesus.' I responded gladly, 'I promise to go and take the "sweets" of the gospel to those people who have been left out.'

And here I was, on my first safari. Here were people who had never heard of Jesus! Right there, in that dry valley I prayed in my heart, 'O God, please take me to those left-out ones, give me many years in Kenya to go on safari to where lost people are waiting to receive the "sweets" of the gospel.' I had no idea of what lay ahead in the years to come.

The stories in this book you are reading tell of those safaris.

An Important Safari

The boys and girls of the school choir were very excited. They were escaping from their boarding school for one long wonderful day, on a lorry to Maasailand!

Some local pastors had arranged this safari to go to encourage a small struggling church there, and they had asked for the school choir to go with them to sing wherever they would preach.

It was quite scary for the school children to go over the border to the wild part of the country where the fierce Maasai lived. It was an adventure they wouldn't want to miss, but they hoped they would not meet any Maasai warriors on a cattle raid. Sometimes they stole girls too! So that meant that I would have to go as well in order to look after the girls in the choir, it was an adventure for me too.

We set off early, before the sun was up. Envious classmates waved us off. The young ones sang at the top of their voices for several miles, until we warned them that they might not have much voice left when they arrived. The ride was rough and the lorry uncomfortable, but that didn't dampen anyone's spirits.

Arriving at the church, everyone was relieved to see that there were no Maasai warriors, just ordinary people like themselves. The girls, however, were puzzled that there were no other school girls to be seen.

Later on after the choir had sung and the people had listened attentively to the preaching one of the local elders spoke to the girls. 'You are very blessed to have the chance of going to school.'

The girls were surprised. Often they did not feel very blessed attending a boarding school, with all the rules and studies – but they knew the value of education and had many ambitions for the future. Some of them had believed in Jesus and were glad of a chance to learn more about their Friend.

'Yes, you are fortunate,' the elder continued. 'Throughout Maasailand there is no boarding school for girls. Fathers don't want their daughters to go to school. The government insists that the Maasai put a few boys in school but there is nothing for girls.'

Our girls were aghast! No girls in school! Why, there were schools dotted all over their own district, with nearly as many girls as boys. Their fathers liked to educate their daughters – they could demand more cattle for a 'bride price' when a girl got married. The more years in school, the higher the number of cows!

Arriving home late and tired, the girls still had enough energy to tell the others in the dormitory of the sad fact that there were no schools for Maasai girls. Most had never even heard of Jesus. They were still living as their grandmothers had lived, while all other girls went on into modern Kenya.

The next evening as I went to the dormitory to have evening devotions with the girls one of the seniors suggested that we should ask God to help those girls to go to school. And so, night after night I heard the girls praying for their Maasai sisters to get a chance of education.

Some time later I heard that the local government, in a district of Maasai far from the one we had visited, was trying to get the Maasai fathers to put their girls in school. The county would fund the building of a boarding school, but the men must fill it with their girls.

The Maasai elders had reluctantly agreed on one condition – the proposed school should be run by missionaries! They wanted their daughters well looked after! However, at that point the Mission said that they had no teacher to fill the post.

I spent some days in heartfelt prayer before responding:

'Oh, yes you do! You have me!'

So the next big safari I went on was the long drive across the country to where this school was being built. At last I was going to people who had never heard of Jesus. I was going to an area still needing the "sweets" of the gospel. I was going to teach girls who didn't know that God has a Son.

I had many exciting safaris while teaching those Maasai girls and then after ten happy years, we left the school to others and started going on safaris to the far away cattle villages out on the plains, to tell the parents of those girls, their brothers and sisters, and many others, about Jesus, God's Son, who loves all of us. Read on!

Teaching Men!

We got into our car for a short but important safari, feeling very uncertain of our role there. We had been summoned, by the local chief, to attend a Maasai elders meeting! It was unthinkable. Women were never seen at the exclusively male gatherings of the elders.

I had taught girls, in a girls-only school for many years. Recently we had started women's meetings, women's sewing classes, classes to teach women to read and write, classes to train girls to teach Sunday School classes. We stuck strictly to our place as women!

The Maasai language favours men. Anything big, important and strong is masculine. Anything unimportant, small, or young is always feminine. A boy is of course masculine, "olayioni", but a small, pitiful or weak boy is "enkayioni" – the feminine gender! So we, as women, knew our place and stuck to teaching women and girls.

Having handed over the care of our dear Maasai girls' school to Kenyan teachers, we found we were still teachers at heart. We had been visiting in an area some distance away and had found out that many of the older girls there had missed out on learning to read. 'Perhaps we could teach them,' we thought. If they learned to read and write it would give us a wonderful chance to teach them about Jesus. The local school teacher was very interested and encouraged us to use his facilities – but then came the bombshell!

'It is not the girls you are going to teach. Our young men have just "graduated" from being warriors. They are now junior elders. They need to settle down and take life seriously. We would like the younger generation, even those who didn't go to school as children, to know how to read, to speak English – to have their say in the affairs of our country.'

We sat open mouthed. 'No, *Mwalimu* (Teacher), men would not want us women to teach them. Just let us continue with the girls,' we protested. But he persisted.

'Next week we are having a big barasa with the elders of our section of Maasai. I will pass on your request to use our school in the holidays and we'll see what they say.'

On the day of the barasa we safaried many rough miles from home, to the appointed place in mid-afternoon. In the very democratic leadership style of the Maasai, every elder feels he must have his say, even if he just says the same as every other speaker. A barasa is a time for great oratory, waving of the sticks of authority, gaining chuckles by using riddles and proverbs and fables of their people. The only things a barasa lacks are brevity, speed – and women!

We sat in our car well out of sight of the elders. We waited humbly for a long time till we started thinking wistfully of home and supper. At last we spotted the teacher bringing the Senior Chief and a few other elders towards us. After dignified greetings the Senior Chief pointed his stick at us.

'You two,' he said sternly, 'are to teach reading and writing. You may use our school building. You are to teach the young men!' We tried, politely, to protest but he insisted.

'You women are not like women of our people. You have no children. No husband has paid cattle for you. You are teachers and we want our men taught. You are the age of their grandmothers, (we were scarcely 40!) and they'll respect you. Teach them well!'

Back home we spent the remaining days writing lessons, getting books and pencils and sorting out Bible pictures.

With our car packed to the roof we made our way to the little school. We set up camp in one classroom. Panes of glass were missing from the windows so it was not snug. Nor were we private. With no curtains we felt like goldfish in a bowl, till we realised that no one lived near the school. Then we felt a bit nervous and isolated!

However, the next morning we were up at dawn, to be ready in time but no one came. We waited a little longer. No one came near us. Some curious children, herding their goats, saw our car and came to investigate.

'No, no one will come here today. The young men have all gone off to fight!' they enlightened us with excitement, as we asked them where the men were.

It turned out that all our "pupils" had picked up their spears and shields to go off and fight a neighbouring clan who were grazing their cattle in the wrong places. Fighting for their cattle's welfare was much more important than going to a reading class.

The next morning however, saw a wonderful sight. Young Maasai men, having successfully chased their enemies off their precious grazing, came striding up to the school, leant their spears and shields against the wall and entered a new world of books and pencils and the smell of blackboard chalk.

Picking up the papers we had put on the desks, they demanded, 'Come, teach us! We don't know what we are looking at!' And so started two weeks of exhausting fun and hard work.

The most popular part of lesson was when the young men would take it in turns to read aloud from the big chart. Now all teaching manuals agree, 'The teacher must never say, "no that is wrong", and must never under any circumstances laugh at mistakes of adult learners'. But they had never met men like these.

They laughed uproariously at any hesitation or mistake of the hapless victim up front, quick to shout a chorus of "meneija!" (it's not like that!) But no one minded the laughing, and enjoyed laughing back at others when their turn came.

The only time they were quiet and attentive was in Bible story time. They listened like children drinking it all in. We had big pictures on the wall and the men enjoyed explaining the pictures to the newcomers, telling their version of the Bible story.

We enjoyed hearing a new version of the Tower of Babel. 'Long ago everyone talked Maasai. But Enkai (God) was displeased with people who were building a high house. God punished them by causing some to speak English, some Kiswahili, and others Kikuyu – so that they could no longer understand each other and so stopped building. But we Maasai continue to speak our language because we are God's favourites!'

A few of the bright ones learnt to read in the two weeks we gave them. Others lost interest. But seed was sown in their hearts and years later, as the gospel spread in their area, some became believers in the Jesus they first heard about, in those wild classes.

Adventure at Leopard River

'Keep going, Grandmother! It's easy! Let's go!' Two passengers were eagerly encouraging me. I hoped the title "grandmother" was a title of respect, not their estimate of my age and feebleness!

I had hesitated. I had driven bravely through the bush, flattening undergrowth and dodging trees, and then found, ahead of us, a wide sandy riverbed with steep sides. The two men - passengers we had picked up on the way, were already a bit disgusted with the timidity of this female driver. We were out looking for a village to visit and they wanted a ride home.

Although we were all eager to arrive, I had doubts about how our elderly VW Kombi would manage in the sand ahead. This Kombi's registration was KAZ 910. As "kazi" means "work" in a local language, we thought that would be a good pet name for this hardworking vehicle.

'Keep going!' they kept egging us on. 'We'll get across if you keep going fast!' Recklessly I followed their advice. We plunged down and ploughed across the dry riverbed until we were nearly at the other side. But as we lost speed, the wheels dug deeper and deeper into the sand and we ground to a halt. Kazi was stuck! We all piled out and started digging in the soft dry sand with our hands while our better-equipped passengers unsheathed their razor-sharp swords and went to cut leafy branches to give the helpless wheels some traction.

'What's that?' I cried out in alarm. We had all heard a low growl from the bushes straight ahead of us, up the bank.

'Oh, just a leopard,' the younger man assured us nonchalantly. 'It won't harm us out here in the open on this sand!' They were so casual about it that we promptly forgot about the leopard and went on digging. We put the branches in front of the back wheels, pushed and revved, and pushed some more. Poor Kazi tried its best but its wheels just sank deeper into the sand.

Then the senior man ordered the younger one, 'You go and call the men from the village to come and push, while I stay here and guard these women. Bring back lots of the straps the women use for carrying their firewood, then we can pull as well as push this clumsy car.'

Not long after the young man left we did what any sensible woman does in a crisis. We made tea. With water, a kettle, a gas stove there were all the necessities for making a comforting cuppa. Then with my thirst quenched I decided to wander up the bank in order to plan out our route once the vehicle was free.

'Come back!' our companion shouted in alarm. 'Didn't I tell you that there is a leopard up there?' Their casual attitude to the leopard's presence had lulled me to carelessness. I scuttled back, duly rebuked for my foolishness.

Hours later, when the dozen or so men arrived, and with much shouting and laughing, had man-handled Kazi out of the sand and up the bank we were eager to be getting home. However, the young man who had fetched the helpers announced, 'I hear you made tea while I was away.'

Visions of home faded as we once again filled up the kettle and because of our lack of mugs and cups boiled a relay of drinks for the crowd of rescuers. The time was not wasted however. We got out the 'box that talks' and the men all bent over it, fascinated. Our strong wooden hand-wind gramophone had eight records of Bible stories in their language. At first it was the novelty of a voice coming out of a box, speaking their language, that caught their attention, but soon they were gripped by the words themselves, as they played the little three-minute messages over and over again.

'We must go now,' I insisted. 'It will soon be dark and I won't be able to find my way onto the road.' But they ignored me. 'We haven't heard the words of that plate yet,' someone protested. 'I want to hear again the one we have just played,' another wailed. Then I had a brilliant idea.

'You two,' I addressed our original passengers, 'may take this box home with all eight black plates. You can play them over and over as often as you like. See that the little children don't play them by themselves. They might break things. When you visit other villages take the box with you and play the little black plates to your friends there also. One day, when we can find our way across your sandy river, we will come back and explain further the words you have learnt.'

Excitedly, they all set off home, waving the prized wooden box with its records, in farewell, as if it was booty taken in battle.

Although we had been unable to meet the people in their remote cattle-camps, they had the player and we knew that they would all go on playing record after record till they were too scratched to be heard, or until the mechanism inside collapsed from overuse. We prayed that those words, like seeds, would grow in their hearts and bear fruit.

Years later we met some young warriors who still remembered the words of those records – they had been children when the player had been brought to their village. Not only did they remember the words but they had come to love the Jesus they heard of on those little black plates.

Scratches Hurt

Scratches Hurt!

I heaved the hindquarters of the third goat into the Kombi and hastily shut the sliding door before another could escape. The frantic climbed inside to cope with her crying baby, a bewildered toddler and her overturned water-can. The three goats had never been confined in a car before. I climbed back into the driver's seat with a sigh, already regretting having offered the over-burdened young woman a lift.

We were setting off on our first safari in our brand new vehicle. We had planned to bring more comfort into our safaris. This VW Kombi was big and strong, new and shiny, bright red and had come all the way from Germany to take us on safari. We thought smugly about all its extras.

Its high fibre-glass-top allowed us to stand upright in it. We had a kitchen unit with cupboards and drawers and a gas cooker, with two burners and a grill, bolted firmly on top. There was a good sized water-container with a tap, installed near the door. The seat in the body was made up of a set of eight drawers to contain all we needed for sleeping-out for several days at a time. The backrest was hinged onto the seat, which folded down to make a lovely big bed. We put in a ceiling over the driver's seat, where we could store sleeping bags and pillows, and another one over the back for mattresses and other necessities.

Our new 'house on wheels' was greatly admired. We promised ourselves that we would care for this brand new car and treat it responsibly.

The time then arrived for us to set off, fully equipped, to visit some remote villages. We were very conscious of the smartness of our new possession. The Maasai would admire it as red is their favourite colour. That was when we met the woman and the goats.

Not wanting to be selfish with the lovely gift God had given us, I stopped to give this woman a lift. She was carrying a water-can on her back. Her baby was tucked tightly in her cloth in front of her, and her crying toddler was trailing behind. She looked as if she could do with help. We exchanged greetings and offered her a ride. When I opened the side-door she gratefully deposited her water-can on the floor and her yelling toddler on the seat. I waited for her to climb in too.

'No, I must run after my goats!' she hurriedly explained as she scuttled off into the bush.

We tried to pacify the toddler but the sight of us white women only made things worse. Three goats came crashing out through the thorny undergrowth at the side of the road, with the harassed woman in hot pursuit. She made a lunge at the nearest goat, grabbed a back leg as it tried to evade her, dragged it to the car and then gathered it up and pushed it inside, where it promptly knocked the water-can over. The jolt dislodged the lid and water trickled out. We now had the task of steadying the water-can and hanging on to the goat, as the distraught woman frantically chased the other two goats. The only one enjoying the episode was the now smiling toddler, clapping his hands with delight. When the mother triumphantly got the remaining two goats into the car we asked her where she was going.

'My home is at Oltepesi, near the Senior Chief's village,' she answered. That was the very area we were aiming for so we took her right to her village. After the goats, water-can and toddler had been extracted she introduced us to all the curious folk who came to see why this great red monster had come to their kraal.

It was easy to get them to gather and listen to our message about God's love for them. After we had been served with huge mugs of smoky milk from the beautifully bead-decorated gourds, we said our good-byes amidst warm requests to come again.

They directed us towards further villages and we set off on a dirt track that presently led us between thorn bushes. We were afraid of getting punctures from the long, sharp, white thorns that adorned every dry twig of these straggly bushes. But the worst of all were the scratches the Kombi suffered on its shiny red sides. We winced at each scratch. They hurt!

'Should we turn back?' we debated. 'We mustn't spoil this beautiful new car!' But we were unable to reverse on that winding track, and trying to turn would take us into more thorns. So we went forward slowly, feeling, in sympathy, every scratch raking at Kombi's sides, as we inched through the thicket.

Once out in the clear, we stopped to examine our lovely no-longer-new car. Sure enough, there were nasty scratch-marks on both sides. We were sorry - its beauty was spoilt, and this was only our first safari!

'Before we find the next village, let's have a sandwich to settle all that milk sloshing round in our protesting stomachs,' I suggested.

But when we opened the sliding door all thoughts of eating disappeared. We had forgotten the mess we would find inside! Spilt milk, leaking water and the droppings passed by the panicking goats! We were glad we had not put carpet on the floor!

As we set to, cleaning it all up, we wondered if we were right in putting our new vehicle into situations where it would be treated like this! It was for carrying missionaries to preach. Did that have to include goats and leaky water cans and messy toddlers? Should we go only where there were proper roads? At least on a road, the kombi wouldn't get scratched.

But gradually, as we cleaned up the mess as best we could, we remembered the village we had visited. The people had listened well to the preaching. Why were they so friendly? Slowly it dawned on us – that getting messed up, and even scratched or hurt, was part of the job. Being helpful, being friendly, giving lifts, going to folks' homes, was the way we would get openings to share the message about Jesus with them.

When we had finished clearing up – though the smell of curdled milk and goats persisted for a long time – we went on to the next village, and the next, and the next.

Several days later, back home, we assessed the damage of scratches, dirt and smell. We also remembered why many of God's people had helped us to get this precious vehicle - to take the gospel to people who did not know Jesus and his salvation, whatever the cost. We had to accept the messes inside, the scratches and the dents on the outside. They didn't really matter, as long as people heard about the salvation God offered through Jesus.

Ambulance for the Aged

'Please, could you squeeze my granny in as well?' This request came from a tall, glorious, warrior, liberally smeared with the red-ochre cosmetic all warriors delight in. He had his arm around an anxious-looking withered old woman whom he was gently but determinedly steering towards us.

We had stopped the Kombi at a large Maasai kraal in the middle of nowhere. It was the height of the dry season, so a cloud of dust had heralded our coming. Once the dust had slowly settled it left everything a dull dingy grey including all the curious people pouring out to us.

Soon we were engaged in the formality of greetings and being mere women, waited respectfully for the men to greet us. While greeting the women we could be more relaxed and informal as we were their social equals.

All the time this was going on, children of all shapes and sizes came bowing, waiting for us to put a hand on their heads in blessing. If we didn't notice them immediately, the little bowed heads would butt us, on stomachs, hips or knees, according to the height of the child, in order to gain attention, and receive their share of the blessing.

We were surprised to find so many people at home. It was mid-morning, chore time, when fetching water or firewood, or herding took most people off onto the plains. The people today seemed busier than usual. Instead of the lazy lethargy the heat and dust engendered, there was lots of bustling activity.

It would be impolite for these people to bluntly ask us why we had come and who we were, so we hastened to satisfy their hidden curiosity.

'I am *Ng'oto Ntoyie* from the Girls' School. I, and my friend here, used to teach your daughters,' I explained. Even if they hadn't sent a girl to school, they all knew about those white women who had gathered girls from far and near for lessons.

'We have come to bring you a message from God,' I added. 'We have this little book here and we want to read to you what He says. Find some time to come and sit in the shade of that tree and listen,' I suggested indicating the only tree, a dried up little bush nearby.

The men talked among themselves for a few moments and then one of them said, 'We are very glad you have come. God has sent you just at the right time.' Our hearts leapt. Were these people ready for the gospel? Had God prepared their hearts? But no, it was neither us, nor our message that claimed their interest. It was the Kombi!

'We are moving today,' they explained. 'As you can see, there is no grazing left in this area, so we are migrating towards the side of the sunset, where there has been rain. Some of the men left early this morning, driving our flocks and herds and we are packing our things on our donkeys and are nearly ready to leave. But your coming has solved a problem we have,' one elder explained at length. 'We have a paralysed man, two sick people and several very old folk who would slow us down – but now we have no problem any more because you will be able to carry them all in that nice big vehicle of yours!'

It did not occur to him to ask us to help them. Were we not women? Theirs to command! Resentment welled up.

Frustration also trickled its poison into our hearts. Here we had come all this way, battling on these shocking roads, to bring them the gospel – the wonderful message of God's love shown in Jesus and they didn't want to listen!

But quickly God's Spirit poured His love into our hearts as He reminded us, 'Didn't Jesus suffer this same frustration? He often longed to teach and preach, but the people were not ready to listen. So instead He just showed them the Father's love in practical ways. This is your opportunity to show them His love. While they don't have time to stop and listen, they are able to see.'

A helpless, paralysed young man was carried gently out to our waiting Kombi, followed by a pathetic little procession of the sick and aged shuffling along, supported by caring loved ones. God's love overflowed in our hearts as we received them tenderly, trying to arrange them, on the floor, on the seats, behind the seats, to help the maximum number to fit in.

Then came that magnificent warrior striding towards us, scooping up his protesting featherweight granny in his arms. She was terrified of this new form of transport. Everyone told him the car was more than full but he melted our hearts by his loving concern for this little bit of "biltong" (dried meat) – his grandmother. We found a tiny space and he gently inserted her and firmly closed the Kombi's door. He spoke to her, through the open window, words that changed her terror to a contented smile. He promised to be waiting to receive her when the car reached its destination – and amazingly, he was!

While we were still settling the quarrel as to which man would squeeze in on the front seat with us, to direct us, our warrior tucked up his scanty cloth and set off at a steady loping run. Soon he was a fast-fading dot in the distance.

Then we set off too, but to our concern, we were told to go in the opposite direction. Nevertheless we obeyed. Crossing dongas and dry riverbeds and manoeuvring between hills, we were comforted to see we were gradually bearing round to the direction the warrior-grandson had gone. We soon came to respect our guide's accurate knowledge of every stone, bush and gully of the vast plains we were crossing.

As we ground our way on and on, we saw a gradual change; more grass and a few puddles in the hollows. Were we finally nearing our destination? Sure enough, presently we spotted some cattle in the distance and some men cutting branches off the thorn trees to make an enclosure before dark.

No dust heralded our arrival this time. We stopped gratefully in the shade of a leafy green tree. The men sheathed their razor sharp swords and sauntered towards us. The little granny peered out anxiously. Then she spotted her beloved grandson edging his way through the group of men. The more difficult short cut he had taken meant that he had arrived in time to keep his promise. He scooped her up again and settled her gently on the green grass, as the other men helped their "cargo" out. They would lie and sleep in the shade, waiting for the others, trudging their weary way on foot, to arrive, hopefully, before dark.

Having fulfilled our function, we were now redundant. We asked for a guide to lead the way back to the road that would take us home. Puzzled, they protested they were all too busy. Why waste a man to guide us over a way we had already come? Would our "footprints" not show us the way? Would we not recognise the boulders, trees, dongas we had so recently passed? They were not being heartless. Actually they were paying us a compliment. Surely we had as much 'bush-lore' and powers of observation as the smallest of their little herders.

We set off cheerfully, and didn't get lost, although we did have to get out sometimes and look for our tracks in the sandy soil. As Kombi's engine got hotter and hotter, grinding in low gear, picking its way carefully towards the far off road, our hearts rejoiced. We had been given a chance to serve, to help in a little way, those aged and helpless but much loved people. We had become part of that village. They would know us and accept us next time we visited that area. Perhaps they would be ready to listen to the message of God's love.

We also remembered that handsome fierce-looking warrior – who loved his little granny, who ran all that way to make her happy. How we wished that everyone would love their grannies as that handsome warrior had done.

A Wedding with a Difference

We had been specially invited to a wedding. Not that the people concerned wanted us there, but because they wanted our Kombi and so they had to include us! Now, if you are thinking of white dresses and veils and orange blossom, you are quite wrong. It was not even the typical Kenyan church wedding. This was a Maasai traditional one, very different from the weddings you are used to, and much more interesting.

Cars are not usually invited to Maasai weddings, not even beautiful red vans. Generally everyone walks, but the bridegroom wanted his wedding to be different. He had chosen the girl, and the family had agreed. He hadn't chosen her because she was pretty. He hadn't even met her. His inquiries mainly centred on questions like, 'Is she an obedient, docile girl? Is her family greedy in the matter of dowry, or would ten cows be sufficient?' Her family was acceptable to his family and that was enough.

He, through his "best-man," had given suitable gifts to the important ones of her family. He had paid most of the required number of cattle for her, reserving a few for when she, in due time, gave him a son. Now his family was all ready to receive the bride. So the bridegroom and his friend, the best man, came to our house for us and especially our car!

'Come on, let's go!' he ordered. 'I am ready.' All he had done was don an extra short calfskin cloak and smear his hair with red-ochre. No tuxedo or tails, or buttonhole in his lapel - only his usual reddish cloth and motor-car-tyre sandals. His best man carried a long elegant milk gourd. Traditionally this was to drink on the slow walk from the bride's parents' home to the kraal of the bridegroom's family, where she would live with her mother-in-law until she built her own house.

The walk is always slow, for two good reasons. However far the journey, the bride will shuffle along, crying. It would be an insult to her family to appear eager to leave them. The crying might just be sham because it is expected but very often it is not as the bride knows practically nothing about the man who is marrying her or, worse still, about the mother-in-law that she will live with. Sometimes it's even worse as there may be senior wives living in her new home who will be waiting to boss her about.

The second reason for the slowness was that the bride was not expected to step over any obstacle in her path. She must just stand, and the bridegroom had either to remove it, or if it was immovable, to pick her up and carry her across.

The bridegroom urged us to hurry, but when Kombi arrived at the bride's village, she was not yet ready – as is the custom of brides all over the world! She was standing meekly outside her mother's house and the women were mixing red-ochre clay with milk fat and smearing it liberally on her legs, arms and face.

Then they brought a wealth of beautiful collars, mostly of beads threaded on wire, in attractive traditional patterns. The bride's mother brought out the special bridal necklace. On this the beads were stitched painstakingly onto stiff rawhide, and hanging from it were more than a dozen long strings of beads, reaching almost to her feet.

We were just thinking how lovely she would look in those colourful decorations, when they were all dumped into the basin of red-brown oily clay, fished out dripping and arranged lovingly around her neck in graded sizes, with the special bridal one on top. We were disappointed to have all this beauty hidden, but everyone else was completely satisfied – that was the way it was to be done!

The final thing to do before she left her village was to have someone pray for the bride. The man who was to pray came with three things in his hands: two gourds and a tuft of grass. He took a mouthful of home brewed honey-beer from one of the gourds, bent over and sprayed her feet with it. Then he stood and prayed that she would have joy in her new home, bearing many children. He then took a mouthful from the other gourd, which contained milk, sprayed her feet again and prayed that she would lack for nothing. Lastly he tucked the grass between the toes of her right foot and prayed for the prosperity that good grazing brings for her future home.

At last ready to leave, she shuffled out behind the impatient bridegroom, tears making dark tracks through the red-clay cosmetic. Then she stopped and stood still. Striding ahead, her husband-to-be irritably demanded that she hurry up. She remained standing. He came back, saw that there was a little stick across the path and crossly picked it up and tossed it away. The Kombi was waiting some distance from the entrance to the homestead, so after that, as he walked, he checked that no more obstacles were in her path.

When she arrived I opened the sliding door of the van. She stood still. 'Tell her to get in!' he demanded of me, but I was on the bride's side.

'No,' I refused laughingly, 'you know what she is waiting for.' Frustrated, he scooped her up and almost threw her on to the car seat and both men scrambled in after her, while we got in the front and started the engine.

'Go fast!' the men demanded, but knowing the custom, I kept Kombi going at a snail's pace, stopping whenever there was a stick or rock on the path, for them to crawl out and remove it.

At last we arrived and a crowd of the bridegroom's extended family gathered just inside the gateway of the kraal. This was the bride's big moment. She walked slowly to the gateway and stood just outside.

'Come in and I'll give you a fat sheep,' a woman called out. The bride looked at her carefully. She needed to remember who had made the promise. 'Come in and I'll give you a black heifer.' It was easy for her to remember this regal patriarch with his red blanket and wildebeest-tail flywhisk.

And so the welcoming invitations and promises were called out to the reluctant bride, till she was sure she was welcomed and accepted. Eventually she felt sufficiently honoured to take the few remaining steps, and so she became a member of her new family. She was led kindly into mother-in-law's hut. She knew proudly that she was a valuable acquisition, bought with ten cows and a variety of gifts - blankets, teapots and many bubbling gourds of honey beer.

We too were taken inside the house of the regal mother-in-law, with almost as much ceremony as was accorded the bride when she was led triumphantly into her future home. We ploughed through over-generous helpings of goat-stew and rice and washed it all down with huge mugs of very sweet tea heavy with smoked milk. They knew we did not drink their honey brew and were glad not to have to waste any on us!

Gradually people, replete with the feasting, wandered out. Children came to admire and also laugh at the distorted reflections Kombi's shiny hubcaps gave. Glorious warriors came to gaze at themselves in the side-view mirrors - smiling widely to view proudly their strong, snow-white teeth, checking on their elaborate hairdos and red-ochre cosmetic as critically as women do in our beauty parlours. Others boldly piled in, hoping for lifts to wherever the Kombi was going!

So eventually we all set off home, the Kombi sadly overloaded, glad that we had played our part. We had done the right thing according to their customs. We had had no chance of telling them of God's love - the adults being too full of the contents of the beer-gourds and the young people too excited by the dancing and singing. But when in the future we went back to those people we would be accepted as friends. The crowds of wedding guests would welcome us to their homes. We had shared in their celebration, and eaten their food. We would one day have the chance to share what we longed to give them. We looked forward to our celebration when they accepted our message and joined their new family, the church.

Then we remembered the 'wedding gifts' offered to the bride. She had been 'given' many things. They were all hers. Yet she had nothing. She had to remember who had promised what, and, when she was in need she must go and claim that gift from the one who had made the promise. How like us! Our loving Heavenly Father has promised us all that we could ever need to live for Him and more, yet often we remain so poor and needy. We need to go and claim from Him all that He has promised to us when we came to Him and joined his family.

The Blind Leading the Blind

'We are going on to Ilmotio. We are trying to find "Ole" Kuraru's village. Is there someone here who could come with us and show us the way?'

We had just spent several hours visiting at Lolpisia's village - a huge circle of about thirty houses. We had sat under a shade tree playing gospel records, explaining them, and telling more if we got sufficient attention from the chatting women and excited children who shared the shade with us. We had given liniment for grannies' aching backs, eye ointment for oozing fly-encircled eyes, zinc ointment for children's scaly heads. Now our stomachs were awash with the large mugs of scalding, sweet milky tea that we had cautiously sipped in Naiputa's house, carefully fishing out the drowning flies! Naiputa had been in our school for several years. She was now married and the mother of many children. She also felt responsible for us.

When we asked for someone to show us to where we wanted to go a buzz of conversation broke out. Yes, they all knew Ole Kuraru's village. But one person was about to go to the shops. Another had a sick child. Yet another needed to go for firewood. 'They all with one accord began to make excuses.' Just like in the parable that Jesus told!

'My father will show you the way,' Naiputa offered. 'He has nothing to do.' She pointed to the thin little old man who, while I had been preaching, had stealthily taken one of our folding stools to sit on. Much to the amusement of all, and in spite of his lack of weight, the long-abused and strained canvass had given way and he had landed, legs in the air, on the thorny ground. Perhaps Naiputa suggested he became our guide to rebuild his shattered dignity - certainly not for his ability as a guide. He was, to all intents and purposes, blind! But we did not know that, and accepted his help gratefully.

We had been to Ole Kuraru's village once before to rescue Kipeno from the threat of an early marriage and had taken her back to school. Once again, she had not returned after the holidays, so we were going to make tactful enquiries about her. We knew that we had to go about 20 kilometres down the 'road', turn left onto a cattle track and again turn left at an unknown spot into the thorn-bush. Having a guide gave us confidence!

'Here is a cattle track crossing the road,' we announced to our rather passive passenger. 'Is this where we turn off?'

'Yes,' he assured us obligingly, not even turning his head to look.

'Are you sure?' we queried cautiously. We didn't want further to shatter his already damaged dignity.

'Did I not herd our cattle in this area as a boy? I know every bush and tree and track around here,' he asserted indignantly.

Glancing sceptically at his scrawny arms holding tightly to the hand-rail in front of him, I replied in my mind, 'Yes, but the trees you knew have long since died, or been hacked down for firewood. Many new tracks have been made and the old overgrown. It was a good fifty years since you were a boy.'

So, with rather shaken confidence, we set off up the scarcely visible track, dodging in and out between trees, avoiding ant bear holes, and praying we would not get more than one puncture from the long double thorns that were everywhere. We had only one spare wheel!

But soon that fragile confidence was shattered completely when he said, 'Let me get out and look around. We may be on the wrong path.' We were not on any path at all, but in our bewilderment we foolishly let him get out to "look around," and he wandered off into the bush.

We waited and waited. And then waited some more! Then it occurred to us with some alarm that half-blind, as we had by now realised he was, he had probably not only lost the path and the village but the Kombi as well! So we gave a few loud toots on Kombi's horn to let our 'guide' know where we were! We were glad to do something, rather than passively waiting. But the 'something' was fruitless. I suggested getting out to look for him. Betty, my fellow missionary, wisely vetoed that sternly. So we continued to encourage Kombi to make loud hooting noises.

After a while, the "toots" brought results, but not what we had expected. Two eager little herd boys came running.

'Where go you?' Asked one of them, breathless from the excitement and running. He scratched around in his sparse memory for the smattering of English he had learned in the two or three months he had wasted in school, before he had managed to escape back to his beloved cattle. They were very amused when we answered in their own tongue and we told them whose village we were aiming at.

'But why are you here if you are wanting Ole Kuraru's village?' they asked with a laugh. But the laugh became uproarious when we explained about our lost guide. 'Naiputa's father is showing you the way? That old man! He can't see! But he can smell! He has probably smelt the beer being brewed in the village near here. He won't be coming back. We'll take you!' The lure of a ride in the shining red monster had conquered any sense of responsibility for the precious family cattle they should be herding.

Arriving at the village they proudly exhibited us, and Kombi, with all the aplomb of a magician producing rabbits from a hat. They felt very important till their fathers noticed them and sternly sent them packing to look after the cattle until dark.

Soon some women recognised us and were eager to hear news of their daughters away at school.

'Have you brought that box that talks?' some eager children asked. They dragged us to the spot where we had gathered on our last visit. Others rushed off calling for their mothers and grandmothers to come and hear what the little black plates had to say. At first some of the children could not tear themselves away from the Kombi, standing gazing at it in admiration. But as the first sound of a song crackled out of the little hand-wound record player they rushed over to another new attraction.

A crowd quickly gathered - children and women sitting on the thorny ground, with men, old and young, staying stand-off-ishly on the outskirts. We played a record, explained as best we could, put another on when we lost their attention, or showed a picture of the relevant Bible story. We told them the story of the lost sheep. We explained that Jesus, God's Son was looking for us, his lost sheep. That he wanted to find us and care for us. They listened well for a while but then the urgent needs of real life intruded.

'The cattle are scattered in the thick bush. The boys need help. It will soon be dark!'

Quickly every male picked up spears and sticks and hurried off. Words might be interesting but not as important as cattle!

Then we tackled the job we had come for. Kipeno must be somewhere, but they would hide her. When a girl failed to return to school we knew that father was keeping her home to arrange for her marriage to the man of his choice. As Kipeno was only thirteen years old we had the law on our side, so I had come to take her back to school. Determined fathers are good at hiding their daughters so I did not ask to see her father but asked some children where Kipeno was.

'She is in another village, staying with her other mother,' they explained.

From that I understood that she was not with her real mother but another wife of her father. A couple of the bigger girls were happy to climb into the Kombi and we went off to look for her. A lovely surprise was waiting for us. She had already heard that we had arrived at her real home, guessed why we had come, quickly changed from her red-ochred cloths and beads and was all ready to go back to school.

She emerged through the gate of the village, a clean, well-dressed little lady in a pretty blue dress. She took us to the home where she was staying and served us tea in enamelled mugs with all the grace that she showed many years later as the wife of Kenya's ambassador to Tanzania and later to Japan.

We had a good time with the people, especially the children of that village, playing the records, teaching some verses and making sure that everyone there knew that God has a Son and that his name is Jesus.

The busy time for the Maasai is just before sunset. The cows return from grazing and the thirsty calves are brought to their mothers for their supper, but at the same time the women come quickly to get milk for their children as well. The kids and lambs, bleating hungrily, find their mothers and plug in contentedly while Grannies grab hold of the other teat and squeeze out some milk for their tea. By the time it is dark, quiet falls on the homestead and everyone is inside.

We invited Kipeno to sleep in the Kombi with us. We were afraid her father might take her in the night if she slept in the village. She laughed at, but also enjoyed, our supper of scrambled egg on toast with a cup of coffee.

Early next morning, we were woken by someone knocking on the window of the car. Our hearts sank. Was it Kipeno's father demanding her back? But Kipeno jumped out eagerly when she recognised her mother's voice... her real mother.

'Is your father very angry with us?' we asked as Betty and I climbed down from the car.

'No,' she assured us. 'He just laughed and said, "Those white women have won this time but I'll catch her next school holidays!"' However, Kipeno's mother seemed excited and kept on saying, 'God is good! Thank you Enkai!' So Kipeno asked her mother why she was so excited.

'In the night I was worried,' she explained, 'that my husband might change his mind and beat me, because Kipeno's wedding plans can't go forward. He has already received a few cattle from the hopeful bridegroom and he doesn't want to give them back. So I thought I'd come early and get a ride with you to the Oltebesi shops to buy tea, sugar and tobacco for my husband. However when I left home, dragging my goat, I had to travel through thick bush. Halfway along I heard a cough and saw a moving shadow – a leopard! Then I remembered how you had said that Jesus, God's Son, is our Shepherd who wants to look after us and keep us safe. I called to him to save me, and my goat, from that leopard. And here we are! Safe and sound! Your Jesus heard me!'

We seemed to fly back home on wings! We had dear Kipeno safely back at school. Her mother had listened to our message with faith. She had found out for herself that Jesus was real, that He was alive and loved her. When the Kombi bounced on the rough road it just felt that it was jumping for joy.

So, the safari when we had a blind man to show us the way, had turned out well after all!

Kombi Accepts Help

We were stuck! Thoroughly and truly stuck. We were also ashamed. People had advised us against this safari. They had told us that our Kombi, with no 4-wheel drive, with a small engine and a huge lumbering body, was not up to it. But we argued that we had often had difficulty in mud – but this safari was through dry desert. The Kombi, we argued further, often had difficulty getting up very steep rough hills – but this safari was through flat country. We were advised to take some men with us in case of trouble, but as we had no thoughts of having trouble we had ventured out alone.

But now we were stuck! Stuck in a little stretch of sand! This shouldn't have given us trouble! But we were in trouble, deep trouble. This wasn't just a layer of sand that sometimes caused a bit of a skid. This sand was bottomless! Every time I made another attempt to get the Kombi forward or backwards its wheels just dug deeper and deeper into the fine loose sand.

We walked for a bit only to find that firm ground was alarmingly far off. We went back and tried to jack the Kombi up to put stones underneath but there were no stones to be seen. Anyway, the jack quickly sank in the loose sand.

We were in trouble! We were several hundred kilometres away from home. No one knew us in this dry land. We were going to visit some missionaries who lived at the end of this "road" we were on, (or in!) They didn't know we were coming and we weren't even sure they were home! These missionaries had come to tell the proud Rendille camel-nomads about the God who loved them, and His Son who wanted to save them. They had found a spring of water up in the hills, had piped the water down, and the concrete troughs below were filled every day. This was a great attraction to the Rendille who were constantly searching for water for their thirsty camels.

When the nomads arrive at the troughs the camels drink first. They drink an incredible amount. The herders drink next. When they are satisfied, they fill the water containers to be carried back to their families. Last of all they wash themselves and their scanty clothing with great splashing and enjoyment. When all the work is done, they love to gather in the cool of the evening to hear new songs, new stories, new thoughts to store up and share with folk back home. We had heard of this interesting work, and had come to see for ourselves.

But would we ever see it? We sat down on the sand. You probably think we should have been digging, or pushing or doing something more practical than just sitting? But we were doing the very best thing possible. We were praying to God, because He knew just where we were. He knew the trouble we were in and He also knew exactly what He was going to do to rescue these two foolish helpless ladies, and their car that had tried its best but failed.

After a while I heard what I thought was a buzzing noise. Could it be a vehicle? No, it was probably a plane high above. Small planes are used a lot by people travelling in this vast and lonely land. We searched the expanse of cloudless sky for the sight of a plane. Nothing! But the sound was getting steadily louder. Hope soared. Was it really another vehicle on this lonely out-of-the-way track?

Yes it was! A beautiful giant Land Cruiser, obviously well equipped for out of the way places! The driver, who turned out to be one of the missionaries we were hoping to visit, was even more surprised to see us than we were to see him. Two stray ladies, far from home, in a completely unsuitable vehicle, travelling on a remote track, stuck in a sandy riverbed that would become a raging torrent if rain fell! A tough guy, used to surprises, he greeted us calmly and we passed the time of the day as if there was nothing out of the ordinary.

Our friend went by the delightful nickname of "Junky" and was well named because, out of the mixed junk stowed away in the back of his battle-scarred 4x4, he produced a goodly length of chain with stout hooks on either end. Furthermore, he had two huge jacks and, with thick planks to put under them, the Kombi's wheels were soon set free. Then Junky hitched Kombi to his experienced "work horse" and slowly but surely Kombi was towed across the sand to "terra firma".

Gratefully, we followed his tracks and arrived safely at their very basic but wonderfully equipped mission "camp". It was really impressive to see the ingenious water system that brought the life-giving water down onto the dry plains. Equally impressive was the meal that was produced that evening, all cooked, (including pumpkin-pie) on an outside wood fire!

The next morning one of the Kombi's wheels was flat; not surprising considering the thorns that adorned every bush and tree growing in that dry land. Our biggest difficulty when trying to mend a puncture, was getting the tyre off the rim. But Junky just hopped onto the great road-grader he had for levelling land for an airstrip. Positioning the Kombi's wheel carefully on the ground, he slowly lowered the huge blade with precision, till the tyre popped over the rim. Removing the tube was the matter of a moment.

A few days later, still blind to how ill-equipped we were for this terrain we were determined to explore further. Knowing that the track we intended to travel had a "lugga" – a short sandy dry river crossing with steep sides – Junky suggested that we go in the 4x4 vehicle that was on the station. But as we decided to go in our own car he gave us a roll of chicken wire and some instructions.

'As you approach the "lugga", get out and unroll the wire across the sand. Drive down gently and make sure your front wheels are on top of the wire. Go carefully across, and up the bank briskly and you'll have no difficulty.' He spoke confidently but I am sure he had misgivings.

We, however, had no misgivings. We set off with confidence and with Gospel Recording records in the local language. We thought we knew what to do.

However, after spreading the wire and carefully driving halfway across, we struggled and ground to a halt. Imagine my dismay when I discovered that the chicken wire had crumpled and twisted around the wheels, around the axle, around anything it could find. Disaster! What could we do? If Junky had been there he would have had wire cutters and all that was needed. But of course he would not have needed them; he would have driven more skilfully!

We prayed. We confessed our foolishness. We called on our Father's mercy and grace to get out of this mess. The best we hoped for was for His care of us till someone came in search of us. We had no food and, worse still, we had no water for the many hours we might have to wait. Probably this track would not see another vehicle for weeks.

Psalm 116 has a very special verse for us. We reminded our Heavenly Father of his word, 'The Lord preserves the simple.' True to his word and full of mercy, he did preserve us!

With amazement we heard the whine of an approaching vehicle – on a road that saw a car only once or twice a month! A Land Rover, packed with policemen, swung round a corner in a cloud of dust! God himself had timed the arrival of this Land Rover. Amused at our plight and feeling very macho, they gave willing and cheerful help. In no time they had us untangled, unstuck and up on solid ground. Then they insisted that we headed home.

Our self-confidence was shattered! How foolish we had been, relying on ourselves and on our Kombi's doubtful strength! But everyone had been kind and had helped us graciously. Yet, I had felt irked at needing to be dependent on others. Of course our confidence should have been, even in practical matters, in our Heavenly Father who is always kind. He truly 'preserves the simple'!

Limping Home

'Oh, good! We will have company on our next safari. Willard is coming with us in his own car!' I called out, as I gleaned this good news from a letter just received. We visualised a strong 4-x4, rugged and tough, available to care for us as well as itself.

We had always trusted the Kombi to tackle terrible roads, or even to get to places that had no roads at all. But after our recent experiences, we realized it was getting older and wondered whether it would soon have to give up the very rough life it was leading. We were now afraid that it might let us down in a remote spot, so we were glad that for our next trip to Loitokitok, on the slopes of beautiful Mt Kilimanjaro, we would have company and we would travel in convoy.

Imagine our dismay and disgust when our friend Willard turned up in a battered little VW Beetle! We felt our roles were reversed and the Kombi would be the one helping, not being helped. At least it would be easy to tow that little rattletrap when it failed to climb the rough steep road to the foothills of Kilimanjaro. Little did we know what would happen!

Willard, being polite, let us go first, and trailed behind in our dust. We proudly forged ahead as we knew the way well and kept looking back to check he was still following. All went well for the first two hours, but suddenly our confidence and pride plunged to an all time low as the Kombi's engine died and we came to a stop. In desperation I tried to start it again but the noises were alarming so I stopped trying. How glad we were that the little despised VW Beetle was following us. Its driver, we knew, was a skilled mechanic. The Beetle nearly bumped into the Kombi, as it caught up with us in a cloud of dust. We were in the middle of the Amboseli Game Reserve, famous for its abundance of the "big five" and an over-abundance of fine choking volcanic dust.

We watched with awe as our hopeful rescuer tightened things and pulled at things until he emerged, straightened up and solemnly gave us the verdict.

'This is very serious,' he announced. 'I'll have to take the engine out. We'll have to get parts out from Nairobi.' Our minds boggled as we realised what this would mean. We were a hundred miles from home, plus another fifty to get to Nairobi. It was only fifteen miles to Loitokitok but all uphill, and very rough and steep!

Our rescuer strolled back to his Beetle, and carefully positioned his car in front of ours. He then got his towrope out.

'Are you hoping to tow us with that little car?' I exclaimed in alarm. 'It will never make it on that rough steep road. The Kombi always has to use the lowest gear to get to the top!'

'You'll be surprised what this Beetle can do!' he boasted. 'It is strong and reliable. I have kept her inner works in perfect condition even though her outside looks a bit old and worn. It will be no problem to tow you uphill. However, your visibility will be almost nil with this dust. Just watch the rope. If it snaps, brake hard! Don't use your brake for any other reason,' he instructed carefully.

The little Beetle groaned and revved, and pulled and strained but kept going, till its driver signalled for a stop to rest. 'It's getting a bit heated. Let's wait to cool down,' he advised. I offered that Betty should walk up the remaining steep part to lighten the load. 'No,' he answered emphatically. 'We need all your weight for ballast. If the car bounces too much on the bumps the rope might snap.'

As we approached the town we caused great amusement amongst the bystanders. We heard one excited boy yelling to his pal, 'Come quickly, come see a mouse pulling an elephant!' We too had a good laugh, as the road was levelling out and the strain and tension relaxed.

We went into the "hoteli" for "chaai" (hot, sweet, milky spiced tea) and "mandasis" (flat, leathery, greasy doughnuts) and felt refreshed. After wandering round the abundant fruit and vegetable market, and visiting the flyblown shack that did as a butchery, we had enough food for what might be many days. We knew that it could be a long time before we got the Kombi back on the road again.

At the vacant mission property the cars were grateful for a rest. But there was no rest for us humans. We set out to make the house, that had stood empty for a couple of years, habitable again. We would sleep in the Kombi, so we made up the only bed in the house for Willard. Later, tired from sweeping, dusting, scouring and making preparations for supper, we went to look for him. But Willard was nowhere to be seen. We called his name loudly as we wandered about. At last we heard a faint answer and followed it to a large shed. There was Willard grinning down at us from an attic. He looked like a little boy who had suddenly found, under the Christmas tree, absolutely everything he had ever mentioned to Father Christmas, with his name on them. And he had!

There were all the things he needed for this current emergency – a well-equipped workshop, with a pit for getting under the car, as well as a block-and-tackle for removing the engine, a large assortment of tools and an attic full of old spare parts that he hoped would fix our poor old Kombi. We had lots to thank God for as we said our goodnight prayers and crawled into our sleeping bags, safe and snug inside the Kombi.

In the morning Willard was once more nowhere to be seen but we guessed where he was. By the time we called him in for a hearty breakfast, he was ready for it. He had Kombi's rather small and inadequate engine out, and was already up to his elbows in grease having taken it all to pieces. With hot water, laundry soap and a scrubbing brush he quickly got clean enough to sit down to a huge breakfast, to give him all the strength he needed.

We were still washing the dishes and cleaning up after breakfast when he came running in, eyes shining, all excited. 'Look what I have found!' he exulted, waving a grease-encrusted, dusty piece of metal. We tried to look excited too, but all we could manage was a puzzled, 'What is it?'

'It is exactly the spare part I need for your Kombi's engine. That part I said yesterday we would have to send to Nairobi for!' He had thought that maybe, just maybe, there might be a part he could adapt as a temporary fix, just to get us home. But there, hidden in all the junk in the attic was exactly what was needed. We marvelled at God's care and thought for our needs, and we praised Him. It took Willard all day to get the Kombi together again. We spent the next day seeing the people we had come to visit and set off the following day, under our own steam, but with the Beetle behind us in case something happened!

That dreaded "something" did happen! Almost in sight of home! We heard a loud crack coming from the Kombi's inner parts; we hoped that it was something minor, like a broken spring. After we explained to Willard about the noise he anxiously examined the little engine and found what he had feared - the engine block had a great crack. Kombi was not just sick this time. Kombi was dead! We were towed slowly home, and the next day in to Nairobi. We put an "on tow" notice on the back of Kombi, but cars passing us on the highway couldn't see the little car that was doing the towing, and several times nearly cut in on us too soon.

We found a second-hand car dealer who bought "dead" cars. He looked at it minutely and then passed his verdict. 'I can't give you much for that old thing. I'll probably use it just for spare parts.'

But he did more than that. Years later we saw our old Kombi, with a new engine, being used to show gospel films outdoors. So our old car was still having adventures, and still helping to take God's message of love to people who needed Him.

A Safari of Surprises

We set off on, what we hoped would be, a very comfortable safari. We were bound for a big mission station to attend our Annual Conference. Friends had invited us to stay with them instead of sleeping in one of the school dormitories. Luxury for a few days, with hot water, electricity and no responsibility! Fresh in our minds, however, was the conversation we had had with an old granny on our veranda a few weeks before.

This dear old woman had flopped down on our veranda step and untied the bundle from her back.

'Ng'oto Ntoyie,' she spoke desperately to me, 'you must help me. My boy is getting too big. I can't carry him any more.' She opened the cloth that was covering her "bundle" and a loud yell made conversation impossible. It was her boy! She quickly covered him again and the noise gradually subsided. I bribed him with a sweet and reluctantly he allowed me to look at him. One leg was withered and his whole body was weak and wasted. I thought that maybe he was retarded mentally, but his granny assured me he was bright, he could talk and he could sing all the choruses that the schoolboys brought back to their village. His weakness came from being carried around on her back all the time – his granny loved him, and was concerned for his future.

'Well,' she demanded, 'what are you going to do?' The ball was firmly in my court. What could I do? We had often talked about the need for a place for crippled children, but our thoughts had, up to then, been mere dreams. She wanted more than dreams.

Faith rose in my heart. 'Old One,' I stated boldly, 'by the time your grandson is old enough for school, we will have a place here where children like him will be able to stay, to be taught to walk and to go to school on their own two legs!'

Having made that rash statement we started praying and talking, but we were completely unable to make plans. We had no idea how this promise could ever be kept but we also knew that if it were God's plan He would bring it about.

That next safari to our Conference, with a stopover for lunch with friends on the way back through Nairobi, turned out to be full of wonderful surprises.

One of the speakers at the conference, an American pastor who had previously given us help to feed many people in a time of drought, called out to us on the last day, 'Let's sit together at lunchtime. I have something to talk to you about.'

We wondered what it could be. There had been good rains that year and we were not, currently, needing to help any hungry people.

'A Canadian group wants to sponsor a ministry to needy children. I have prayed about it and God has told me to give this help to you.' he explained,

'But we don't have any project with children at the moment,' we protested. However, he was completely unmoved. 'If you don't have a children's ministry now, you soon will. God has clearly told me to give this to you,' and he handed us a cheque, with the promise of a similar amount every month.

On our way home we stopped for a lunch date with Robbie and Rosemary, English nurses who had a mobile clinic that did safaris into Maasailand.

'We are so glad you have come!' was the warm welcome we received. 'We have something we want to talk to you about.' That sounded familiar!

Over a delicious lunch, they gave us their news. They had received a generous gift from a company in Nairobi towards their medical work with Maasai children. Now they were thinking about how best to use this help.

'What we would like, is to put up a small building where we could keep children for a while. Often we find a child needing an operation. We come to Nairobi to look for a charity bed, or a kind surgeon, but when we go back, the village has moved and we can't find the child. Our trouble is that we have no plot in Maasailand. We wondered if your Mission would erect this building on your mission station, and we'll use it for needy children.'

By this time, our mouths were hanging open with surprise. All these things were tumbling over each other, to make sense. My promise to the old granny! The needs of many children! The gift from Canada! God's guidance of our American friend! The cheque already sitting in Betty's handbag! The generous gift from the Nairobi firm! And now, this idea our friends had of a building for needy children! God certainly wanted that wild promise of mine to be honoured!

By the time we parted from our Nairobi friends, plans were whirling around in our heads. The Nairobi firm's money could provide the building. The Canadian money could feed the children and pay for a couple of Maasai Christian women to mother them. We would do the organizing and supervising. Our nurse-friends would bring the children, find treatment for them and bring them back to us for further care.

So that is how the Child Care Centre at Kajiado came into being. God, with his beautiful compassion for handicapped little ones, brought two South Africans in touch with an American, who had contact with some Canadians. He added two English ladies who had a gift from a firm in Nairobi - all to answer the cry of that granny with a crippled grandson.

In the next story you will hear how he added some Germans and a Scot to complete the picture. Isn't our heavenly Father clever!

Crumbs on the Carpet

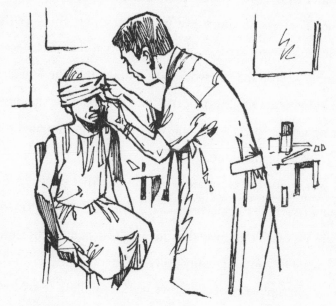

A motley crew piled into the little box-like Suzuki jeep!

Our Child Care Centre was now running at full steam but today's safari was to an eye-clinic, run by a German Christian mission, at a hospital just outside Nairobi. Of the children in our care, there was one handsome boy who was completely blind following measles, another was a small boy who had a skin disease that was spoiling his eyesight; one little girl was dreadfully cross-eyed, and others were short sighted.

Once we arrived, most of the morning was spent sitting in long queues. Everyone around us was talking a language we didn't know. But when we actually got to the doctor, his assistant met us with a broad smile and a greeting in the Maasai tongue. There is so much eye trouble amongst these cattle people because of the flies and the dust, that the doctor was training a Maasai man to work with him, so that the Maasai-speaking patients would not be frustrated by not understanding or being understood. While our party was being examined we chatted to a German nurse.

'I work with the German based Mission that ministers to people all over the world who have eye troubles,' she explained. 'We are especially interested in helping any people with eye problems. Do you have many other children like these?'

'No,' we replied reluctantly, 'we have only these few. Most of our children are polio victims.'

At that she became even more excited. 'Oh, how wonderful!' she beamed, 'My brother has just come from Germany to start a project to help physically handicapped children.'

Our hearts leapt and our minds reeled as she persuaded us to take the opportunity.

'Go and see my brother today,' she urged. 'I'll phone him now. I'll tell him you're coming. I'll give you his address. No, he won't mind entertaining your whole car-full. He is eager to meet people just like you.' She overrode all our protests and early afternoon saw us driving into a posh Nairobi suburb.

We were entertained royally and were soon talking wildly of a Land Rover, a Nurse's house, money for salaries, funds for this and that. The children, sitting on the floor, happily spilt their cool-aid and scattered their cookie crumbs all over the deep-pile carpet. Our hosts were nobly unconcerned about the mess we left behind as we went off home rejoicing. God had added a German brother and sister to the team that he was gathering to answer that granny's cry.

By the time the Child Care Centre had been running for a month we were exhausted. We had spent many months, finding building materials, coping with builders and with all the unexpected hassles along the way. It was an exhausting job choosing and training Christian Maasai women to care for the frightened children and comfort them.

'You two go on a holiday to Mombasa. Go and rest, we'll come and stay in your house for two weeks.' These words from our two nurse-friends from Nairobi were music to our ears. They would do their out-clinics in the area, and at the same time sort out the health needs of the children! We packed up gladly and had a lovely holiday at the Coast. While there we met Georgie, a Scottish missionary who was having a break while she waited for her Kiswahili Language Course to begin in Nairobi.

Perhaps unwisely, she mentioned to us that she was a bit bored just waiting. We thought of all sorts of ways to relieve her boredom! 'Come to Kajiado,' we invited her. 'We can give you lots to do!' Perhaps the good Lord clouded her usually sane judgment. So instead of palm-fringed tropical beaches, and azure seas she had a pile of jobs donated to her by two lady missionaries greedy for help!

Georgie tackled all the jobs we gave her willingly. She went off to her language-learning course. Would that be the last we'd see of her? No! She came back. She came back to take over the running, and all the worries of the Child Care Centre. So that is how Georgie, a highly qualified midwifery tutor became a self-taught orthopedic expert, who has helped hundreds of handicapped children through the years. Many like Kumoin, the old granny's little charge, have had operations on their weak legs, been fitted with braces and crutches and taught to walk, to go to school and even to play football.

Children, and handicapped ones especially, are right on the top of our Heavenly Father's list of important things to see to!

Late for Church

'Aaa! Huh-Huh! Eeii!' The little deaf boy, the last of the many children we had piled into the vehicle earlier that morning, was shouting loudly and waving his arms like a windmill! Sensing it was some urgent message he was trying to give us, we stopped the Land Rover. How were we going to know what he was telling us?

This was a Sunday morning, and we had set off in the Child Care Centre Land Rover with a long list of errands to be done. We had been invited to speak at a church fifty miles down the road. So we also took the opportunity to carry some sheets of corrugated iron needed for finishing the little house that was being built for the pastor there. School holidays had started so, in return for the use of the Land Rover, we were to deliver the deaf and crippled children whose homes were on, or near, the road we were travelling. They had climbed into the Land Rover excitedly, little suitcases and crutches being tossed in after them.

Several times along the way we had made a detour into the bush, to take a child to their home. This caused great excitement. A Land Rover coming to their village! One of their own children arriving home in state! It was time for celebration, so we were invited to go in and have a drink of milk. Visitors must never leave a Maasai home hungry.

Gradually the noise level in the car lessened as we left the children one by one, in their homes. Finally the only one left was the little boy who was profoundly deaf and could not speak. But hurrying along the road, anxious about the time, we suddenly discovered that he could make a big noise when he needed to! We stopped the Land Rover and tried to find out what the trouble was.

He made the matter known to us very clearly and dramatically. He pointed to the top of the Land Rover, he waved wildly and pointed back down the road. We knew immediately what had happened. Some of the corrugated-iron sheets had blown off and were now somewhere far back on the road. We first tied the remaining sheets more securely. Then we turned and went slowly back down the road, looking carefully as we went. Three-yard-long iron sheets, shiny new, should be easy to see. But we found nothing. After a long way, we turned and came back up the road feeling puzzled. Where could the roofing be? We soon found out!

A man waved us down. 'Have you lost something?' he asked us politely.

'Yes,' we explained. 'We were carrying roofing for the pastor's house at Namanka. The rope broke and some flew off. We have been back looking for them. But we have failed to find even one.'

'How many blew off?' he asked us. When we said we didn't know he asked us to count the remaining ones. It took some time, and we were getting anxious about being late for church. But he insisted on knowing the exact number that had been lost.

'Do you know where they are?' we asked, wondering why he wanted to know how many were missing. He laughed.

'Yes, I saw them come off. But women from that village in the bush over there also saw them and rushed to collect them and hide them. They were hoping that you would not come back! Let's talk to them.'

We walked with him into the village and he greeted everyone politely, and then explained our visit.

'Mothers of this village, these women want their mabati that you are kindly keeping safe for them,' he announced tactfully. It would be unwise to accuse them of stealing! 'They thank you for looking after those seven sheets of mabati that got lost and will give you each a few shillings to express their thanks.' How we praised God for sending such a wise man to get our iron sheets back! I would probably have been blunt and caused offence and left without the mabati being revealed. As it was, I bought them all back at ten shillings apiece and we parted friends, everyone happy.

We looked anxiously at our watches. It was way over the time for church to start, but things are often late in Africa, so we hoped for the best and hurried on. Rounding the last corner we could see a crowd of people standing outside the church.

'Oh look!' I rejoiced. 'They are gathering to start the service.' We drove up with a flourish and tumbled out – only to find the service over, everyone saying goodbye and setting off home.

The deaf boy was happily reunited with his mother. The young pastor was glad of the roofing for his new house. The pastor's wife had lunch ready for us. Everyone, except the missionary ladies, had done the right thing! We had not been in church to worship the Lord with that congregation as had been arranged.

We agreed, then and there, that Sunday is for going to church! We could have taken the children to their homes the next day. We could have had more time in each home and shared more about God's love with them. We could have had a good time of fellowship with the Christians at the Namanga church.

It certainly is better to do each job one by one and do each one well.

The Elusive Tankful of Water

'This will be a nice easy safari,' I remarked. 'Travelling with Stan, all the hassles will be his.'

And that was exactly what happened to poor Stan – all the hassles were his!

It was also an exciting safari for us, as we were going to be starting a new mission to the Njemps people, a Maasai speaking tribe, who knew very little of the message of God's love. The local government chief had allocated us a site on a rocky hill overlooking Lake Baringo. It was in an area that was cut off from the little "civilisation" that there was in the district, by three bridgeless rivers. That did not worry us as our experience of rivers in Kenya was mostly of dry river courses that very occasionally had flash floods, and soon dried up again. Little did we know what trouble those rivers would give us in the years ahead.

We had stopped off in the city to buy a small petrol-driven water pump and a hundred feet of strong black rubber hose. Before we could think of any building, or even being able to live there we would need water. As our home would be on the edge of a cliff overlooking the lake we reckoned we would be able to pump lake water up into a tank for our use.

After our last visit we had arranged with the chief to employ some men to clear bushes and rocks from around the footpath and it had happened! Six of the seven volunteers had completed the work and had done it well, so we praised them, paid them gladly - and offered more work for the next day. We asked after the seventh volunteer and found out that he was in hospital. We expressed sympathy.

Each of the men excitedly added his bit to the explanation. 'Oh, he is not ill!' 'He was just mauled by a lion.' 'He has been sewn up.' 'He'll be back next week.'

I enquired nervously whether the lion had been on our hill and if it was still at large. We were planning to sleep in tents!

'Oh, no. He killed the lion but got a few scratches doing it. The lion killed one of his cows right near his home. He was so angry that he was rather clumsy. He should have killed the lion with one throw of his spear,' a workman explained, to comfort us.

In the meantime we were eagerly awaiting the arrival of two large corrugated-iron water tanks to be brought out on a lorry, together with a load of cedar posts, and some timber. When the chief heard of this arrangement, he looked very doubtful.

'Don't come to work until you hear the "voice" of a lorry. It may be many days before it arrives,' he told the men.

Soon after this the chief mysteriously disappeared. We had hoped that our water tanks would arrive the following day. Would the chief's suspicions be right?

The men helped us put up our tents and advised us to take any heavy things we had out of the car and put them in the tents. 'Why?' we queried. 'Would they not be safe in the car?'

'Oh, it is not the safety of your goods we are worried about,' they explained. 'It is you yourselves we fear for. The wind is so strong at night here that your tents could be blown away with you inside them!' So, as well as our luggage, we weighed down the tents with several of the good-sized stones that littered the hill. The men, by now good friends, promised to come in the morning to see how we had fared, whether they heard the lorry or not. Our tents did not blow away that night. Though in days to come they blew down several times, they never quite blew away. They got torn in the process but Betty mended them skilfully.

At the crack of dawn Stan was off to the cliff searching for a route down to the water for the rubber hose. He cut down bushes and dislodged rocks. Suddenly he appeared, red faced, breathless, running uphill as fast as he could. A buzzing swarm of bees was after him, angry at being disturbed. Stan rushed into his tent and zipped it closed.

The men, who had just arrived, were not sympathetic. 'The bees will only sting if you wave your arms about, or if you run away. Just stand still, they will walk on you but they won't sting you,' they advised. After we had anointed Stan with what remedies we had, they all went off together.

'If you have to run from the bees,' they advised him further, 'don't run up to the tent, run down into the water.'

Later, two of the men came up to fetch the pump, a can of petrol, some oil and a spanner. 'Stan is going to start pumping. He says you must watch this top end of the hose and wave to us when water appears.' Quite a while later we heard the chug-chug of our brave little pump and kept our eyes eagerly riveted on the hole. We watched till our eyes squinted – but nothing came out. We kept waving down the sad news and they kept trying.

After a while the little pump stopped and a band of weary, discouraged and thirsty men arrived. We had anticipated their needs so had a huge pot of tea ready - real tea called "shaai" made in the Kenyan way. Tealeaves with lots of milk and sugar are all cooked together to make a heavy nourishing brew.

So we, all eight of us, settled down to a late breakfast of tea and bread spread with margerine. The food and drink ministered to the thirst and tiredness but nothing helped the discouragement. Why could they not get the water to the top end of the pipe?

Stan sat glumly paging through the users manual of the new pump. And then learnt the bad news. The pump could raise only sixty head of water – meaning it would pump water to the height of sixty feet only. And our cliff was just over a hundred feet high!

Our spirits rose when we heard the "voice" of a lorry grinding its way up our hill. The chief, smiling broadly, jumped out of the passenger seat and announced triumphantly, 'I have brought everything you ordered!' Then we realised why this dear man had disappeared the day before. Knowing the tardiness of the suppliers in the little town and the difficulty of getting transport for the goods, he had hastily left us and walked the three-hour shortcut to the town. He had used his persuasive powers and authority to great effect. He managed to get the merchants to supply the cedar-posts, timber etc. with only the promise that the next day some unknown white strangers would come and pay them. He also made a tour of the government departments to find a functional lorry and eventually talked the Water Department into letting this lorry and a driver go on the worst road in the district – all with the promise that they would be paid for the fuel the next day!

'I've also found a fundi for you!' Now, that word "fundi" means an "expert" in any practical, artisan skill. But as the word is most commonly used for builder, we rejoiced that the chief had brought someone who could erect the framework of our little house, and pour a concrete slab. When we came back it would, hopefully, be ready to add the wooden walls and the roof. It was only much later, when the poor fundi had made a mess of the framework, and achieved an eight inch slope on the concrete slab, that we learnt that he was indeed a fundi - but in the mending of bicycles and transistor radios!

The men and Stan set to, carefully lowering the water tanks to the ground and stacking the timber well on a platform of stones – the hungry termites could consume wood in an alarmingly short time. We regaled the chief and driver with tea and bread - but in all the activity the problem of the water cast a pall on everything. Suddenly something dawned on us!

We had not known that there would be this problem, but God did, and He guided us to get two tanks. We had thought that this was so that we had one for building needs and the other for our living. But now we could put one tank halfway down the cliff and the other at the top and our brave little pump would be able, in two stages, to get water right to the top.

Stan and the chief climbed down the cliff to find a suitable site for the tank and prepared the surface to receive it, while the men were doing the same for the other tank up top. The driver drove off happily and I sat down with the fundi to explain what he was to do in our absence. We measured, put pegs in where the posts were to be planted, wrote it all out and I asked him about tools. He assured me he had all the tools necessary – what he meant was he knew where he could borrow them!

The tank was manhandled carefully down to the site prepared, halfway down the cliff. The pipe was cut and put into the mouth of the first tank, the pump was taken down to the lake and after what seemed an age, water, beautiful water, (clouded and smelly water but beautiful to us at that triumphant moment) came spurting into the first tank.

When, after an even longer time, the first tank was full, they hauled the pump up to the half- way station, and repeated the tedious pumping process. It seemed hours before the tank was full to the brim and the poor overheated pump could rest. Its persistent throbbing voice was silenced, and quiet reigned.

We had more tea - thirst quenching tea, for Stan and his patient team. As they sipped the tea they teased Stan about the bees. But they also congratulated him that he had, in the end, managed to let the bees walk on him without panic. When the stew and rice, being cooked for a very late lunch at 5o'clock in the afternoon, was ready, we all ate in tired silence. Satisfied, the men drifted off to their homes, and we relaxed, with a hard job successfully completed.

While we were sitting chatting in the cool of the evening, we heard a loud slurping noise. Betty and I were alarmed. We remembered the lion – and wondered what wild animal was sharing our beautiful hill. But one glance at the look of horror and dismay on Stan's face, told us what the noise was. All the water, pumped up with such effort, with much patience and so many bee-stings, was gone – siphoned down the hill, simply, by gravity! With a shocked despairing look, he hurried down the path to inspect the other tank halfway down the cliff. It too was empty. One of the men, thinking of the safety of the hoses, had pushed each right to the bottom of the tanks to keep them safe!

Poor Stan went to bed early. He was up long before dawn and we woke to the chug-chug of our valiant little water pump, doing yesterday's tasks all over again. It took hours to refill the tanks, so it was in the mid-day heat that we struck camp, packed up and set off on the long journey home.

Stopping at the little town, we went to pay the trusting supplier for the tanks and timber. We found the water department and paid gratefully for the transport. But most importantly for Stan, we found a dingy little eating-house that had a fridge! Before he drank the three cokes he ordered, he finished off a large jug full of ice-cold water. With the itches and swellings of his many bee-stings we thought it wise to go to the local clinic, where he was given a shot of something, which didn't help his discomfort much.

Poor Stan! We were sure he would never help us again. But, a month later, with the bee-stings long since faded, he was all ready and eager to make the journey once more.

He was an example to us – he could take difficulty and discouragement strongly and with patience. We didn't know then, that more of that was awaiting him on the next safari!

Don't Forget the Transformer

Our Suzuki jeep, which we had named Suzie, looked very small. The lumbering Land Cruiser and the huge Hilux overshadowed her and made her look like a Dinkie Toy! Suzie was piled with luggage inside and out. She was doing her very best to play her part to the full in this safari, but her loads could not compare with the huge heaps of boxes and bags of belongings that those other monsters could carry.

Suzie was a little third-hand Suzuki 4x4 jeep, just a small square box on four wheels with a tiny but valiant engine and, at the moment, completely flattened springs. The sticker on the back saying, "Load should not exceed 220 kilos" was completely ignored. At last, we left Kajiado, where I had lived for twenty-five years, to start the long safari to our new "Home on the Hill". Suzie valiantly led the way, with the other vehicles groaning along after her, despite her lack of size.

In Nairobi we stopped to buy a small portable, petrol driven generator. The second stop was in the next town, to load on our newly acquired fridge and two large cylinders of gas. We travelled on for several hours on potholed tarmac. Our final stop along the way was at the last outpost of civilisation. There we loaded up with a pile of juicy paw-paws, a whole stick of bananas, several loaves of bread, huge cabbages, a whole bag of potatoes, and many other things needed to feed the workers and ourselves when we set up home.

We were sad to leave the place where we had worked for many years. We were also a bit scared about what might lie ahead in the unknown area to which we were moving.

At last, shopping over, we turned onto a rough dirt road, flanked by huge acacia umbrella trees on one side and lush banana and papaya plantations on the other, and then, suddenly, we came to a river.

Now, in the area where we had worked for a long time, there were many places that we called rivers, but they were just sandy riverbeds. Water flowed only on the day it rained and maybe for a few days after a very big rain. We had never actually seen them flowing because the roads also became impassable when it rained. However, we realised with awe the frightening effects of those rivers, as we saw the huge dongas gouged out by the water and the enormous trees uprooted. Here was a proper river, a real river. A river with water flowing! A river of water of unknown depth, flowing across our road!

Outwardly brave, I got out, took off my shoes and found a stout stick. I stepped timidly into the water. I wished it would stop flowing, like the River Jordan stopped when the priests, carrying the ark, put their feet into the water. It didn't even notice my little presence but kept on flowing happily. By the time I was halfway across, the water hadn't reached my knees so I reckoned Suzie would manage it safely. Back at the car I was alarmed to see how high up on Suzie my knees reached but I kept my fears to myself. I drove gingerly into the water and Suzie did well. It didn't rush and splash its engine or go so slowly that it got bogged down. We were relieved to arrive safely on the other side.

The other cars caught up with us and at last we arrived safely at the site of our new home to be warmly welcomed by many local people. The three cars had done their job well, so they settled down to a well-earned rest while we humans got to work. We put our belongings in the wooden store which had been built on our previous visit. Then we cooked supper on a camping-gas burner, lit lamps and discussed our plans for the next day.

The "fundi" had done his job. The posts were standing, more or less straight. The concrete slab looked a bit wavy but not too bad. The timbers were in place for receiving the weatherboard. The men were eager to start, early in the morning, to cut and nail on those boards to make the walls of our house. The eagerness was partly because it became very hot later in the day. But the real reason was that they had brought their toys; their wonderful tools that made any work seem fun and easy to do. That is why we had bought the little generator – power for these fancy tools.

So, after a quick pre-breakfast of coffee and burnt toast, they eagerly got out their tools and went off to work. The generator was British made and the tools were from the USA, but they had a good transformer.[1]

---

[1] Generator is a machine that supplies energy when there is no power available. A transformer transfers electrical energy supplied by the generator to other pieces of machinery that require this power to operate.

'Ronnie!' Stan called out. 'Just go to my car, will you. The transformer must still be in it.' Ronnie came back with a worried look.

'It's not there. Let's look in the other cars.' But their faces grew blank with disappointment. With their power tools the job was a breeze; without them, a long hot slog.

Glumly, they measured and marked the timber ready for sawing. But at just the right moment their breakfast was ready. As they ate huge bowls of cereal, we finished frying the bacon and eggs, and again burnt the toast and our fingers at the open fire. However, even a bountiful breakfast, finished off with pawpaw and bananas, did little to raise their spirits. They set off despondently to sharpen the clumsy handsaws that they had not expected to use.

As they cut and nailed on the boards, they very soon discovered that the "fundi" who had poured the floor slab, either didn't have a spirit level or had no idea how to use one. In the length of the building, only twenty-feet, there was an eight-inch slope! However, they carefully put the boards on horizontally, and left us to worry about the gap at another time. Every time they struggled with handsaws, hand screwdrivers and cumbersome bit-and-braces, they mourned for their transformer, left far away at home.

But they completed the job in spite of weariness, blisters and aching arms. After chatting quietly in the slightly cooler evening air, Stan prayed before we went to our tents to rest.

'Father, we had a hard day today, because of our carelessness. We left our transformer at home. We had to struggle in our own strength. This has taught me a lesson, Father. Sometimes we struggle and fail because we have forgotten your presence, forgotten Jesus our Transformer, forgotten the Holy Spirit, our source of power. Help us to remember that in Jesus, through your Spirit, you have given us all we need to live and work for you. Thank you Father, Amen.'

The next day those men left us. The two big strong vehicles went back home. Just two fearful ladies and one tiny Suzuki remained. But God our loving heavenly Father was with us. Jesus our true "transformer" was with us. Whatever would happen in the days to come, we were not alone.

Little did we know what would happen the very next day!

The Safari We Didn't Go On!

'Those hardworking men have finished all our food!' I called out to Betty as I peered into our new, now near-empty, fridge. Meagre leftovers were all I could see. The fruit and vegetable baskets had a few wilted remains.

So we decided that we needed to go to the little town, back across those three rivers, to replenish our supplies. We also needed to get more petrol, not only for the Suzuki, but also to keep the generator going to give us light, and for the pump that supplied us with water.

In our store I found that each of the four jerry cans had only a few drops of precious petrol remaining. I started carefully dribbling this from one container into another, when suddenly the whole world exploded and I rushed outside. Hungry flames were spreading, threatening everything. What had happened?

I had forgotten that our little gas fridge had a naked flame. The fumes in the shimmering heat of the metal shed had ignited. Very soon the fire spread to the all the inflammable contents of the store. I yelled to Betty to bring water. But the little we could toss in from the doorway just sizzled ineffectively. We dared not try to save a thing. The rubber hose attaching the fridge to the gas cylinder, very soon burnt through and the contents sprayed out. The innocent little store turned into a fiery furnace, reminding us of Daniel's three friends. We retreated to what we hoped was a safe distance. The spare filled-to-the-top cylinder of gas was standing in the middle of that inferno. We waited anxiously to see what would happen. We soon knew!

With an ear-splitting bang the cylinder exploded! Adding more fuel to the fire inside, it dramatically burst through the tough metal roof, a ball of fire. Where would it land? Suzie was to one side, our tent was frighteningly near, and our half-built wooden house was in a very dangerous position.

It landed, after what seemed a long moment, near enough to the car to give us a big fright. It quickly burnt out, ending as a pathetic skeleton of twisted metal. Truly our Heavenly Father was looking after us. We were not hurt. Suzie was safe. We still had our tent and our soon-to-be home.

The huge volume of black smoke and the loud explosion alerted the local people who came running to help, and stayed to comfort us. Some children stood around Suzie and stroked her dusty sides to comfort her. We saw a group of our new friends talking in a huddle and looking worried.

The Headman approached us. 'Will you be leaving us, now that you have had such a bad trouble and have lost so many of your things? The people say they would be very sad if you went.' So our all-wise Father was already using this accident to make us accepted and wanted. We changed from being the rich outsiders who could perhaps exploit them for our own profit, to shocked ladies needing their care and comfort.

'No,' we assured them, 'God has sent us here! We can't run away just because of a few troubles. Thank you for coming up the hill when you saw the smoke. Thank you for your concern for us. It makes us know that we have come to good, kind people. True, we have lost some things, but our Suzuki is safe. Our tent with all its contents could have been destroyed. The beginning of our new wooden house could have been burnt up in the fire. God has kept us all, safe. We would like to say a special "thank you" to God tomorrow.' We turned to the Headmaster of the little school below our hill and asked him if we could use a classroom as "church". He readily agreed and turned to all the bystanders.

'Please, will you all come to the school tomorrow morning. Tell all the other people to join us too. I will ring the school bell loudly. When you hear its voice you'll know it is time to come. (The bell was a two-feet long piece of railway line, hung up on a tree, hit vigorously, using a piece of iron piping - it had a very loud "voice".) Tell everyone that we want to welcome the "ladies on the hill". They want to say thank you to Enkai for looking after them in the fire. Let us all gather to praise God together with them.'

So the church at Kiserian was born the next day. Many people came. They listened well and sang along with the school children the choruses they had learnt at school. They listened with interest, mostly because they were amused at my speaking Maasai, which they understood basically but with many differences of dialect. But something of the message we brought sank in. Like all newborn babies, this infant church was not strong, and didn't know much. But, for the first time many mothers and fathers came with the children on a Sunday morning to praise God for His love and care, and to hear for the first time, about God's Son, Jesus Christ. Over the weeks some lost interest, new ones came, till there was a regular core of those learning seriously the truths of the wonderful gospel story. After a year, on the church's first birthday, ten men and eight women were baptized in the muddy water of the lake, as a testimony of having been changed by Jesus.

So, after all, we had not forgotten to bring the Transformer – the real one – Jesus, the true Transformer. He had changed a bad happening, a dangerous fire, into an unexpected opportunity to start the task we had come to do, on the very first Sunday we were with our new friends. We trusted Him to continue to transform many of those people into His true followers. And He did!

The Ugly made Beautiful

Women, the world over, love babies, especially tiny newborn infants. They love to coo over them, to coax a smile from them, and proudly try to decide whom in the family they might resemble. Maasai women are the same, only they show it differently. They spit on them! Or rather, they spray them gently with the spittle of blessing, as God's blessing comes to us as rain, rejoicing in God's miracle of a new little life.

But, when Jonathan was born, his mother tried to hide him. She was ashamed. She had borne an ugly child, a child with a cleft palate. The young mother wondered what she had done that the Great Enkai, the Giver of life, had given her a baby so spoilt, so ugly. When women came to see the baby she would just say that it was asleep. Her mother-in- law, of course, knew what was wrong and gently prepared people. After a while they came and cooed, sprayed and blessed him, but nothing removed the shame from his mother's heart.

Jonathan was four years old when we settled in his district. Severe drought had come to the area. One day when we were checking on all the children to enrol them in feeding centres, which later became nursery schools, we met this little boy.

We sat with Jonathan and his mother and the chief and talked about taking the little boy to our mission hospital to have his lip repaired. We told them about a very skilled plastic-surgeon who was visiting Kenya for a month to repair the lips and mouths of as many children as could be found – and he would do it free of charge. The chief talked wisely and comfortingly to her, removing all her fears till she agreed to the operation. By the time we were ready for the journey, we had two more candidates for the operation – two young schoolboys from a few miles away, whose parents had never before heard that there could be help for their children.

Naishorua, our new red Suzuki jeep, was happy when the day came to go down country. This was just the kind of work for which God had given it to us. Which was why we gave the jeep that name - it meant 'that which was given'.

Jonathan's mother was going with the three boys. None of them had been far from home before. All of them knew only their own language, which was not spoken at that hospital. They were all silent and frightened as we set off, until we stopped for a snack - bananas and milk. After that there were many new and interesting things to see along the way. They grew bolder and happier as the hours passed.

'We will come back after a week to take you home,' we explained to our little party. They looked at us as if we were throwing them to hungry lions, but we left them in the care of a well-run hospital and skilful doctors. We knew they would be cared for. After some wonderful days back in Maasailand, visiting many people who had been our friends in years gone by, the time came to go and collect our group and head back home.

'We have come to collect the three boys and the mother we left here a week ago,' we explained to a sister in charge.

'Oh, yes,' she answered, 'I am glad you have come. They are very excited. They have been happy and have healed well, but they are looking forward to going home. Go down that passage,' she pointed, 'turn to the left and you'll find them in the children's ward.'

We went. The ward teemed with children of various shapes and sizes, all dressed in hospital gowns. We couldn't tell which were boys, much less recognise those boys we had brought to the hospital a week before. They were mostly rushing round, racing wheelchairs, and chasing each other. We didn't want to admit we didn't know our own children! We were ignored. Their games were too absorbing. We went back and asked the sister who had helped us before.

'Where is the young woman we brought, the mother of the little boy called Jonathan? Could you find her for us please?' At least we would recognize Jonathan's mother, and she would be able to find her charges. But when she came it was quite hard to be sure she was the right person. Someone had given her a pretty floral dress to wear and a week of cool healthy climate and lots of hospital food to eat had made a new lady of her. But fortunately she knew us, and bustled off to round up the boys.

Three beaming, handsome little boys came and greeted us. We looked in amazement. They had been so ugly and shy. Now happy, confident, good-looking lads came to travel home with us. Jonathan's mother just kept on shaking her head in wonder and repeating, 'Supat Olaitoriani,' 'The Lord is good,' over and over again.

As we hurried back I thought about the joy of the families and playmates when they finally saw these changed boys. I thought of our Heavenly Father who also rejoices when even one boy or girl finds Jesus as Saviour. He takes away the ugliness that is in us and makes us beautiful inside.

A few weeks after this, a woman arrived at our house. We guessed who she was. Her young son, one of our newly-handsome boys, stepped from behind her where he was hiding and proudly presented us with a basket of lovely fresh maize cobs, the first fruits from this year's harvest.

'We have come to say thank you for taking Lolim to that hospital,' his mother explained. 'We are very happy that our son is healed and whole. All our family are now attending the new church at Sokotei. Lolim told us that it was people who believed in Jesus who had helped him so we should follow Jesus also.'

We prayed that all that family would soon be made as beautiful inside as their son was changed on the outside.

As we chewed on fresh "corn-on-the-cob" for supper we praised our Heavenly Father that He can take away the ugliness that is in us and we can be made beautiful in His sight, through Jesus!

A Kind Man and a Generous Lady

A smiling young man came towards us. We shook hands solemnly. We were strangers, but felt a kinship. Then we heard beautiful words from him.

'You seem to be in trouble. How can I help you?'

We beamed at him and sighed with relief. Our Suzuki, heavily laden, had been climbing the Eburru Mountain for hours. We had started on the dry dusty plains. As we climbed higher, the countryside became greener and the roads wetter. We passed through lush farms with fat dairy-cows, ten-foot high maize, flourishing potato fields alight with purple and white flowers, hard-working people and hordes of children who waved happily at us as we went by.

But still we climbed. The road was badly eroded on the steep parts and deeply muddy on the few level patches. I spied a fork in the road to the left.

'That is the road to Paulina's house!' I cried out confidently. We had been to visit that lady once before, but someone else had been driving that day. However, it looked familiar and we were longing to arrive. We had promised to show filmstrips at her home in the evening. Paulina was to call all the Dorobo people around at sunset to see the pictures.

But as we drove along the road, it became less and less familiar. It also became less and less of a road. When we arrived at a flat grassy shelf cut into the mountain we decided we must turn round and go back. But how? An almost perpendicular maize field above us, with a frighteningly steep drop below and a very narrow space between, wasn't a nice place to turn! We climbed out of the car – and saw to our horror that we also had a flat tyre. The road was so rough that we must have been going on it for a good distance without knowing.

Our rescuer, whose name, he told us, was John, politely suggested that we start by changing the wheel. A good idea obviously, but also welcome as it delayed the task of turning.

John was helpful and handy and soon our first problem was solved.

He must have been a very brave man. He went to stand on the brink of the abyss. With arms waving and fingers pointing, he encouraged me to get the car turned safely.

'That is two of your problems solved. Now for number three. Where did you plan to go when you got lost?'

'We were going into the forest to visit some Dorobo. Do you know a little hunchback lady called Paulina?' Most people despise the Dorobo, especially these hard-working Kikuyu. But our new friend's face lit up.

'Oh, I know Paulina!' he said. 'I was at her home last week. People of our church have been visiting the Dorobo homes and she is the only real believer we have found. I'll come with you to the place where you took the wrong turn.' We went off together and then, with much warm handshaking, we parted at the corner. We went on our way, praying we would not have another puncture.

It was late afternoon by the time we arrived at Paulina's home. There we found a number of women busily peeling potatoes in her house. We were given a warm welcome, as well as an even warmer mug of tea to drink, served from a huge "suffuria" containing enough tea for an army. More women kept arriving. Each brought a basket full of potatoes and gratefully accepted a mug of tea. I wondered, 'Was Paulina running a teashop? Or was she serving tea in exchange for potatoes?' I was glad we had brought her a gift of sugar and a large packet of tea. But it was all very puzzling.

When she explained to us what was going on, we realized that it was really our fault! We had asked her to invite all the Dorobo who lived nearby, to come and see the filmstrips. A hostess can't invite people without having a feast for them. Potatoes, at this high altitude, are the main crop and so also the main food. Tea is the universal drink for those who don't brew stronger stuff. Boiled potato, with onion and curry powder makes a warming supper on a cold rainy evening. It was getting colder as night came nearer and just as we thought of going outside to see where we could set up the projector, near enough to where the car was standing, to use its battery as power – it started to rain. A deluge, a storm, a downpour!

Everyone who was outside crowded into the small two-roomed house. The wooden-shuttered windows were tightly closed against the storm – but of course, also against the fast-fading daylight. The only light in the main room was the fire. The only lamp available was sent to the other room where many men were huddled. All the benches and stools had already been put there for their use. The women sat on the now rather muddy floor.

In the flickering firelight it was fascinating to see the production line at work. Two women served large helpings of potato onto plates. These were passed on across the room, from hand to hand, into the men's room. Another group served and passed mugs of tea along the line, also to where the men were eating. After a short while, empty plates were sent back and handed on to two women who had another production line – washing, drying and handing back to the servers, to do the whole line again. There were only ten plates and twelve mugs for the large crowd, but somehow, eventually everyone was fed and watered without anyone moving!

Someone, tentatively opening the door, found that the full force of the storm was waning and a few went out into the wet world to make way for new arrivals awaiting their supper.

By the time we managed to emerge and set up our projector the rain had stopped. Normally everyone would have happily sat on the grass and all would have been easy. As it was, no one could sit down. We put the screen under the eaves of the grass roof. Behind the standing crowd a helpful man held the little projector high above their heads, while Betty reached up to turn on to the next picture. I stood next to the screen to tell the story of the pictures that only a few of the audience managed to see. But that put me under the drips from the grass roof. Drips that accumulated to be rivulets of cold water running down the back of my neck! I had to shout to be heard above the constant noise of one half of the audience asking the other half what they had seen. A slight breeze would bring down a shower of drips from the trees above us. Then everyone moved about and complained, while I paused to get their attention again.

Not much of our message got across that evening, but it was a wonderful time of making friends. We had huddled together in the storm, shared food and discomfort, had laughed and grumbled together.

People started drifting off and we looked forward to a good night's sleep. But we noticed many others making their way into the house. These were the latecomers who hadn't yet had their share of the feast. So it was some time before we were at last left alone with Paulina and her three daughters – she had chased her husband off to sleep elsewhere. She refused to let us sleep in the main room. We might feel lonely! She and her daughters arranged some benches in their shared bedroom and put a rather doubtful mattress onto it. That was our bed for the night. We tried to wash and undress, but found it difficult under the interested eyes of three giggling girls. Lying down cautiously we just fitted and wouldn't fall off as long as we remembered to turn over at the same time.

We spent a long, disturbed, itchy night and got up, washed and dressed early before we once again became the entertainment of three amused little girls. But soon the morning became a repeat of the evening before! Our "bed" once again became the seating in the main room. People streamed in and devoured platefuls of potatoes and never ending mugs of tea.

'Who are all these people who have come this morning?' we asked our overworked hostess.

'They are those who couldn't come last evening because of the storm. You said you wanted to meet all the Dorobo who live in this area.' Poor Paulina! She had to feed all these people from her very slender means just because we had carelessly mentioned wanting to meet the Dorobo community!

We went home humbled by her generosity, warmed by the acceptance we had gained amongst these reserved Dorobo people, and ashamed of our thoughtlessness. We also examined our sleeping bags, relieved them of certain invaders and hung them in the warm sunshine. We never repeated that kind of safari, for our hostess's sake, but also for our own!

Downhill is Easy

Naishorua, our red Suzuki jeep, must have been feeling very ashamed of herself. She had let us down seriously! Or perhaps we were at fault for making her do more than she was capable of doing.

We were excited. We were going on safari to visit a new church, in a new area where we were starting a new ministry, travelling on a very old road.

Remember, Naishorua was a small car, with limited space and strength. Sheldon, the strong tall missionary whom we were teaming up with in this new work, was travelling with us

– his car didn't have 4x4 and low ratio gears. So we asked him to take the wheel. He agreed so I sat in the back and admired the way he treated Naishorua gently over the bad patches, and coaxed her up the steep parts.

'Put her into first in the low-ratio gears for this hill! She'll make it!' I advised our able driver, uncomfortably squeezed in behind the steering wheel. We had come to the last hill before the land levelled out at the top. Not only was it a steep hill but muddy, with deep ruts where lorries had churned their way up. Naishorua would have to go very, very slowly and her three passengers gave her a heavy load to carry.

The gears slipped in easily and we held our breath as she climbed, inch-by-inch, in and out of ruts, doggedly pressing up towards the summit. We all shouted 'Hallelujah' and 'Well done!' as we arrived triumphantly at the top, and stopped to give our little jeep's over-taxed engine a well-deserved rest. We got out to stretch, then piled back in eagerly, ready for an easier ride and the new group of Christians we were soon to meet.

Gently moving the little lever to put Naishorua back into the ordinary gears, it arrived at "neutral" and stopped and refused to go further. He pushed and pulled and wiggled it in every direction but having arrived in 'neutral' it had decided to stay there and nothing could change its mind! Thoughts of church faded. New thoughts such as, 'What do we do now?' crowded into our minds instead. The only traffic using that road were the lorries coming to fetch the potato crop. But it was Sunday. None would come today.

After some minutes of foolish worrying and puzzling, we did the sensible thing – we prayed. We asked God to help us, to show us what to do. And he answered! No, he didn't heal our Naishorua – her gear remained in the position it had stubbornly chosen. He didn't send a mechanic dropped from heaven. But an interested passer-by pointed out some far-off wheat-fields where a huge combine-harvester was "eating" its way though a field of golden wheat.

'A company has brought three harvesters into the area to hire out for cutting the wheat, and they have a mechanic to keep those monsters going,' the passer-by explained. The word "mechanic" was music to our ears. Sheldon nobly set off on foot, on what we all knew would be a very long walk, first to ask the driver of the harvester where the mechanic was and then to persuade him to help us on his rest day.

It was several hours later that we heard the roar and clatter of a rattly wreck of a breakdown truck. We were glad to see our companion but even happier to be introduced to the mechanic. Soon he was delving into Naishorua's works. But, used to working on huge machines and tractors, he despised our dear car's littleness.

'This thing is a toy! My tools are too big. My fingers can't get in where they should go,' he grumbled. But he persevered for three hours, finding the fault and finally fixing it. Church time was long since over so we drove home, nursing our jeep all the way, changing gears gently. We got home safely and when we checked with a mechanic in town, he pronounced that the gears were working well – we could do the trip again without fear.

Two weeks later, with me driving this time, we climbed the hill again trusting that the low ratio gear system was in working order. The climb was successful - but with the same result!! The gear lever would not budge out of neutral. This time poor Sheldon knew what to do. He set off on foot and eventually found the mechanic. But he was ill, with a very high temperature, suffering from malaria.

However, Sheldon had negotiated with the driver of a tractor and plough to tow us homewards. We were a bit nervous at the idea of being towed, and the rather ragged looking ropes to be used did nothing to allay our fears.

The men decided that our jeep could go downhill on her own "steam", and would only need towing when she ran out of impetus on the level, or came to the next hill. It was rather scary as they turned the car and pushed her to the top. Sheldon rode on the tractor to keep a watch on us and communicate with the driver. True, it was easy to go downhill. Too easy! She soon gathered speed and we had to curb her on the very rough, rutted road. We were afraid, with no gears holding her in check that we would burn out the brakes. We were quite relieved when the road levelled out, and we slowly came to a stop.

We waited for the tractor to catch up with us. They tied their ragged ropes to the front and with a jerk we were off, advancing steadily up the incline. At the top they untied us and we freewheeled down again. This happened over and over on this up-and-down road. Twice the tractor driver stopped to pick up a couple of passengers who clung to any available part of the tractor. Anything for a free ride!

Then it started raining! Sheldon and the four hangers-on all jumped off the tractor, yanked the back door of our poor car open and jumped in. Now, instead of dust, a thick spattering of mud was being thrown on the windscreen. The wipers tried their best but couldn't keep up with the amount of mud being thrown up. Just then I felt the rope snap and I braked desperately to stop us running backwards. We slithered sideways into a ditch. The extra weight of the men in the car had caused the rope to break, but we were also glad of their presence. It took the strength of all the men to manhandle us back onto the crown of the road.

Going up the next rise, the rope snapped again and was knotted once more. With each knotting, the gleaming, sharp ploughshares got nearer and nearer. It was with great relief that at last we arrived home safely.

'Yes,' I thought that night. 'It is easy to go downhill. Just let go and down you travel, faster and faster. How much harder it is to climb, to keep going upwards. How much help - pushing and pulling, I need to keep going upwards.'

My thinking turned into praying before I fell asleep. 'Lord Jesus, please keep me from ever letting go and slipping backwards, or letting go of my faith in you and rushing away downhill. I want to keep climbing, going upwards, going forward, in my safari with you.'

Soon I was asleep, dreaming of dust, of mud, of slipping and sliding and glad of that strong tractor pulling me ever upwards.

Narianta at Last!

We had tried to get to Narianta several times before by travelling along the slope of the Eburru Mountain until the track petered out and we had to turn back. At one time Sheldon had accompanied some Dorobo believers on a preaching safari, climbing down the cliffs to get to Narianta, but there was no road from that direction. On his third attempt he took another route, carrying roofing materials for the new church, but was again defeated within a few miles of his destination. All he could do was unload at the forestry office where the track ended, and send a message to the church leader.

This was the fourth attempt and we were with him. We went miles out of our way on the flat dry plains to approach Narianta from the other side of the mountain. When we started climbing the foothills we came to lush gardens of the hard-working Kikuyu, who, if they had as much as two square yards of land, would get potatoes growing, plus a good stand of maize with beans climbing up the stalks!

The steeply sloping fields, shrouded in hedges, left just narrow gaps for "roads." We squeezed our way through, ever upwards. As the roads got steeper, so they grew wetter and when we felt we were fairly near our goal, the rain came down in earnest. We slithered and skidded in the very lowest gear, but when we saw an even steeper and wetter road ahead we gave up and went home.

Months later we heard that the Forestry Department had made a road, or at least a way through to Narianta. There was illegal felling of trees in the dense highland forest with its magnificent timber giants. The road, which had been made in an attempt to stop the thieving and destruction, was of great help to us – and we could now reach Narianta!

Having two overseas visitors, we felt that a safari to that elusive place was the best way to show them what was meant when we stated in a letter, 'we went to church last Sunday'. No one could imagine the hours of travelling involved, to get to a place a mere twenty-five miles away!

The first few miles were dull for our visitors. It was another matter as we started climbing, and entered the forest. Here the road never dried up. Deep ruts made by the pirate timber-lorries didn't fit the wheels of our sturdy 4x4. Several times hoes and shovels (always carried in case!) were put to good use by the two young men of the party, to fill in the deepest of the ruts. Then we ran into a huge flock of sheep coming down from the highlands. One sheep ran off into the forest, and of course all the rest followed. It must have taken hours for those unfortunate shepherds to gather them and calm them in that unfamiliar, dark forest.

Later, when the road was even narrower, steeper and wetter, we met a herd of cattle. No scattering for them! They just stood and glared at us. The young Maasai warriors came running to guide their beloved cattle. Our car was perilously near the edge of the road. Beneath us was a steep drop, far down through the tangled undergrowth. With whistles and comforting clicks, the warriors skillfully guided their cattle on the narrow gap between the forested mountainside and our car teetering on the brink. They got them past us safely.

When we arrived at Narianta it was more than worthwhile. The excited new believers greeted us with smiles and hugs. They sang to us and then took us into the home of Daniel, the church leader. We drank tea and chatted until we heard the church bell – an old plough-disc, suspended from a tree, being hit energetically with an iron bar.

As we walked to the newly built little church, I noticed the visiting pastor searching the ground where a felled tree was being chopped up for firewood. He selected a rough piece of wood and hid it in the bag that held his Bible. I reckoned that it was going to be part of his sermon. But I wondered what parable he was going to find in that rough bit of wood.

After much singing, reading and praying, that pastor was invited to preach through an interpreter. Sure enough, he took out the piece of wood, gazed at it and showed it to the congregation. 'Does anyone want to buy this from me?' he asked the puzzled listeners.

'No,' they laughed, 'it is of no value! Throw it away!'

'No, I won't throw it away! It is of value to me. I chose it specially. I like to carve animals out of wood. I love to change bits of useless wood into something beautiful and of value,' the pastor explained. At that he delved into his bag and took something else out. He held it up and the people gasped.

There was a delicate carving of a lion, head stretched forward, stalking its prey, about to make the killing sprint!

'This was also once a useless bit of wood,' he explained. 'I chose it. I planned what I would make of it. It took many days of carving and smoothing and adding the finishing touches. But in the end I successfully shaped it into what I had planned. All of you here in this church today, you who have recently believed in Jesus, God chose you. Some people might think you are not important or of great value. But you are, to God. He chose you. He has started to make you into what he wants you to be. He is shaping you, changing you. Sometimes his knife might hurt, but he will go on until you start to look like his Son, Jesus. That is why he chose you, why he chose me – so that we will, in some way, become like Jesus – loving, kind, pure, faithful people. He wants us to show others what Jesus is like so that they will believe in him also.'

The way home was easier. The road had dried slightly and we were going downhill. I sat thinking of that little piece of wood and wondered how the Great Carver was shaping me? Did I still look like the old chunk of wood, or was the shape he planned for me starting to show. I am so glad we had been able to reach Narianta in the end. The sermon was worth it!

Kirragarrien Adventures

Reversing up a muddy, slippery, rutted track, so steep that I had to grind up in the lowest of low-ratio gears, is not my idea of fun. I am hopeless at reversing. One day a stranger, idly watching this lady driver reversing down a narrow lane between flowerbeds, remarked, 'I could do better than that, and I don't drive!'

One Sunday, Musanka, the leader of a small church we were visiting, was late for the morning service. He arrived panting and apologetic. 'Sorry I am late! I went to take some food to my mother yesterday afternoon. It is not very far but it took me four hours to get there. Even coming down this morning it took me much longer that I thought it would.'

I pricked up my ears. We were in a new area and needed to find all the areas where the Dorobo were living. The Rift Valley was steep and thickly forested. I jumped quickly at what I thought was a good idea.

'Musanka,' I offered, in my ignorance, 'next time you want to visit your mother, tell us and we'll take you in our Toyota. If you took four hours on foot, it should take us just half an hour by car, even if it is a very bad road.' I wondered why he looked a bit doubtful about my kind offer.

Well - I soon learned my lesson. On the day that we went it took us five hours! The only track that a vehicle could go on went up and up, then along the escarpment and dizzily down again! We slithered down expecting to cross a stream and tackle the incredibly steep last stretch. We were within sight of Musanka's mother's little house, but were forced to leave the car and walk the rest of the way. That took us much longer than we expected. We went slipping and sliding, but on arrival we had a lovely time, talking with her about Jesus and drinking huge mugs of tea. Afterwards we slithered back down to the car, the mud helping us to get down in record speed.

We had left the car facing the little creek, the impassable obstacle that had forced us to walk. There was no way I could turn that Toyota short-wheel-base Land Cruiser. Maybe the car could do it but certainly not the driver. The "road" was just a small cut in the soil. The cliff side was muddy and eroded. The other side was an invisible drop down an unknown distance into the forest.

So I was forced to reverse up that track we had slithered down. I would never have managed it but for the patient, gentle encouragement of a young man whom we had found waiting for us at the car. He bravely, or foolishly, followed the struggling 4x4 up the hill, watching my wavering ascent anxiously. He mimed the direction I should turn the wheel. Only letting me know the danger by his eyes opening wider and wider, the size of his eyes mirroring my nearness to the precipice! But his encouraging smile never faded, till we were at the top, the road was wider and we were able to turn.

We hoped then that we were on our way home. But we were stopped, at the command of my rescuer, to visit his grandmother. This lady, Mary, my rescuer explained, had heard about Jesus and had believed in Him years ago when she was working on a farm down in the valley. She was, he explained, the only one in the community who followed Jesus. She had seen us going by and had heard that there were missionaries in that car.

'She sent me,' our rescuer explained, 'to find you and ask you to visit her. She says you must visit because she is calling all her neighbours to come and hear the wonderful message that changed her life years ago.'

Soon I had to pinch myself. I could not believe what was happening. I was preaching to an attentive crowd of Dorobo tribes-people, at the home of a dear Christian lady whom I had not even known existed. My dear rescuer, still determined to care for me, stood behind me, holding a big rain umbrella to shield me from the equatorial sun. Later we listened with wonder as the village leaders decided on a more central venue where they would meet on the following Tuesday. 'You are to come and tell us more of the words in that book you are holding!' It was a command we were more than glad to obey!

That turned out to be the beginning of the Kirragarrien Church. In the months that followed we had many, many safaris to this place. Some people accepted Jesus into their hearts. Some of the young men came down to our training centre to learn to lead this new church. We had exciting safaris to help them put up a building. The local people donated posts and timber from trees they culled from their own land.

Some kind Christians of another area donated corrugated-iron sheets for the roof.

On one of the building-days, we brought a team of missionaries who had some rather modern gadgets such as chainsaws and special equipment for digging holes.

The local men quickly downed their blunt handsaws and Pangas in amazement to watch the visitors' chainsaws cutting logs as if they were banana plants. But those short logs, when planted in the holes, became legs for the new church pews. As soon as good strong planks were securely nailed onto the legs, people scrambled for a place to sit – proud of the seats that they had made. It was easy that day to gather the people to listen to the preaching – they were all already sitting waiting.

How we prayed that those people would continue to come eagerly, Sunday by Sunday, to hear about Jesus, God's Son, and to believe and follow Him.

Good Samaritans

The biggest adventure was still to come. The time was ready for the new believers to be baptized. I didn't drive on that occasion. Sheldon was going to do the baptisms and the communion so he and another visitor from overseas were getting a lift with us. We all crowded into the jeep along with their wives - so it was a tight squeeze.

The rains had wrecked the already bad roads so instead of a safari that usually took two hours, we had to take a huge detour of over a hundred miles and approach Kirragarrien from the opposite direction.

But at least we were sure of getting there!

Famous last words! Within just a few miles of our destination, our driver splashed recklessly in to a bad patch of standing water, and in a moment we were stuck! When he couldn't go forward he tried to go backwards. In vain! We were hopelessly stuck.

Sheldon took off his footwear and waded through the mud. 'Try again!' he shouted to the visitor who was driving at the time. The moment the engine roared and the wheels spun, he spotted the problem. Trucks had ploughed through that water, making deep ruts. Our poor Land Cruiser, now more of a "Water Cruiser", was grounded, its tummy firmly on the hump between the ruts.

We all reluctantly climbed out. The driver hoped that without our weight in the car, it would manage to slither forward.

But no! As the engine roared again, all four wheels spun madly – like a paddle-steamer stuck on a sand bank.

People of another tribe whose language we didn't know, looked on in sympathy and said, "Sorry", before they walked on to their own church! Nasty thoughts of "Pharisees" passed though my head.

Just then we heard a vehicle approaching. I called out, 'Oh, here comes the Good Samaritan!' The driver of the pick-up did all he could to help us but, even with all the men pushing, we remained grounded.

Much to our annoyance, the other driver easily found a way to by-pass our sea of mud. If only we had gone that route instead, we would have been at our church service by now. However, the other driver gave the four ladies in our jeep a lift. The two men waved sadly to us as we left them – still hoping that some help would miraculously arrive!

We had an arrangement with the believers to meet them at a place along the road where a stream was dammed up, giving the perfect situation for baptisms. But when we arrived, no one was there. Not one person, yet we were already very late. The two other women decided to hike up to the church to see what had happened. In the quiet of the forest, with just the rustle of leaves and the soft tinkle of the little stream, we washed our muddy legs, donned our footwear, prayed for the men at the car, and for the missing congregation.

After what seemed like hours, we heard voices in the distance. Heralded by children running down the hill, the whole congregation appeared, singing as they came. Knowing how wet the roads were, they had decided to stay up at their church until they were sure we had arrived!

We had a happy time, praising the Lord, listening to those who were to be baptized tell us how Jesus had changed their lives. I stretched out my sermon, hoping that at any minute Sheldon would arrive to carry out his part of the service.

He eventually appeared, limping on sore, blistered feet. With his shoes wet and feet muddy, he had decided to walk barefoot. It was probably a relief to him to get into the cold mountain water to baptize the radiant believers. We were just finishing the hushed communion service, sitting in a cathedral of soaring trees, on pews of lush green grass, when the Land Cruiser came bumping up the hill, driven by the triumphant overseas visitor. We crowded round him to hear the news.

He told us how those "Pharisees" had come out of their church, had again looked in sympathy, had again said "sorry" and just walked past. But, within a few minutes they were all back, changed out of their Sunday clothes and armed with shovels and hoes! They quickly got to work, skillfully digging trenches to drain the water away. Then, with the hump now visible, they dug hard at it till the car had its wheels on the ground at last. Then it was easy to drive the car onto dry land. He thanked them and tried to give them money for their help but they shook their heads vehemently. In signs, and words he couldn't understand, they explained that they loved God

– so they had first gone to church. But after that, they had come to help their neighbours. They proved to be true Good Samaritans!

I repented of thinking of them as Pharisees as we passed them, on our way homewards. We waved to our Good Samaritan helpers as they recognized the car and they waved back. Children from everywhere came rushing down paths to add their greetings. I realised then that one didn't need a common language to recognise God's true children, the Good Samaritans of this needy world.

Safari Rally Adventures

All these adventures you have shared with us were just our own private safaris. But there were, in East Africa, other organised, exciting motor races called 'The East Africa Safari Rally.' If you don't mind being covered in dust, with scratchy eyes and a mouth full of grit, the East Africa Safari Rally is a wonderful adventure – for drivers and spectators alike.

This tough three-day event, with top rally drivers from all over the world speeding along the most appalling tracks in East Africa, used to be held over Easter weekend. That is the best time for a really exciting race, as it is just when the dry season is due to end and the rains are expected. Maybe they could go on practice runs, speeding confidently on dry dusty, corrugated tracks, but in the real race find themselves churning in deep mud, and slithering down new-born rivers.

Sadly the date has been changed to February, the hottest, driest season. So there are no longer any surprises. It's just dry and dusty and all that the spectators see of the racers is a thick cloud of dust speeding by.

'Have you ever thought of entering for the East Africa Safari Rally?' a nervous passenger asked me with a twinkle in his eye. I was crashing a Land Rover over a rock-strewn riverbed, rushing up a steep muddy bank and then weaving in and out through bushes, narrowly avoiding ant-bear holes. He was impressed that this middle-aged woman could handle that rough terrain at what he thought was a breakneck pace. Little did he know that, had I been a rally driver, I would have recklessly flattened the bushes and jumped over the ant-bear holes at twice the speed. Speed and luck are the name of the game in the Safari Rally.

One year we were in Loitokitok, a little border town on the slopes of beautiful Mount Kilmanjaro, when the Safari Rally was due to pass through there that night. The rains had come with a vengeance and two of our teachers had been stranded at school when the Easter holidays started. No bus or "taxi" would venture on the flooded roads. So we foolishly offered to take them the ninety miles to their homes in Loitokitok in our little VW Beetle!

Miraculously, slithering or wallowing, according to different depths of mud, we made it all the way, without being overcome. However, we were eventually stuck in deep mud right outside the home of one of our passengers. The teachers, thankful to have arrived safely, rallied their families and friends and we were soon pushed to firmer ground. We zig-zagged our way further up the hill to where a missionary couple lived. They received us graciously, gave us afternoon tea and showed us to their guesthouse and left us to rest.

'But they haven't said anything about supper,' we whispered to each other with concern. We had had a hard journey, no lunch, a cup of tea and a couple of good homemade biscuits. We hoped that their hospitality included meals!

There was only a double bed in the guesthouse. It was so well sprung that if one of us moved, it rocked – which gave us a fit of giggles and made the bed wiggle more. Eventually we gave up trying to sleep and decided to go and see if there were any prospects of supper. We chatted to the lady in the kitchen but no mention was made of us sharing the stew she was cooking, the smell of which was making our hungry tummies rumble.

She called out to her odd-job man outside, 'Please go to the garden and pull one carrot. Wash it and bring it to me.' Our hopes plummeted. One carrot was not going to contribute much to that stew to make it enough for four hungry adults. But when we saw the size of the carrot he brought in, we were comforted. In good time, we shared a satisfying meal with our new friends. The rich forest soil sure grew things big.

'The first Safari cars are due around eleven o'clock tonight,' our host told us. 'Would you like to go down with us to see them?' We accepted the offer gladly and everyone went to bed very soon after supper, to put in a few hours sleep first. Our full tummies helped us forget the rocking bed and we slept soundly. In due time, our new friends knocked on our door loudly, supplied us with rugs and jackets and we rode down with them a short way, to where there was a checkpoint.

We gazed into the darkness. We knew that there was a vast plain down below, but there was not a glimmer of light. Then we spotted a pinpoint in the distance, then later another, and another. The road, we knew, was dead straight as it followed the pipeline taking water from the snows of Kilamnjaro to the railway. The cars seemed to be crawling, but we realised they must be coming at a tremendous speed for us to be able to detect any progress. The first rally cars were on their way!

Then suddenly the whole scene changed. The heavy rain-clouds parted and a glorious full moon broke through, flooding the world with a soft silver light. We tumbled out of the car to glory in the beauty of the moonlight.

Our friends called out urgently, 'Come back! A lion was seen in the town a few days ago!' We took no notice however. Many folk were drifting down to the checkpoint and we reckoned there would be safety in numbers. We gazed down at the car lights, like an uneven string of beads moving across the plain. But we were puzzled. One by one the first lights disappeared! Then we realised that the cars were near the mountain now, starting to climb towards us, hidden by the curve of the road.

'Look behind you!' someone called out. Remembering the warning about a lion, we turned quickly and then gasped, not in fright, but in wonder. The clouds had dispersed and Kibo, the highest peak of Mount Kilmanjaro, shone silver and ice-white in the moonlight. We gazed in awe at the splendour, the vastness and the beauty of God's jewel that is so often shrouded in cloud. We gazed and gazed and Safari cars checked in and set off again – and still we gazed.

Eventually we came to our senses and showed a little interest in the rally cars. Finally we went back to bed for the rest of the night – to dream, not of racing cars, but of moonlight and snow-capped summits.

We heard the next day on the radio that the cars had met a particularly badly flooded area just a few miles on from Loitoktok. Some were almost submerged in deep watery mud and had to give up the race. Others managed to bypass the quagmire and made it into Tanzania.

During another of those Safari rallies we had a very exciting, but frightening, experience. We were travelling on a remote pebbly road when suddenly a passenger shouted in alarm – 'Pull off the road! Quickly!'

Without thinking, I pulled off the road into some vicious looking thorn bushes. With a deafening noise, a safari car whooshed passed us at breathtaking speed, showering us with pebbles. It was all over in a moment, but had we still been on the road it might have actually been "all over" with us, and the car. We sat in shocked silence. Then we sighed with relief and breathed our thanks to God for his care.

The passenger who had warned us, explained, 'I had heard on the radio, that rally cars were practising in this area today. I noticed a cloud of dust along the road. It was moving so fast that I guessed it must be one of the Safari cars.' We thanked him warmly for saving us.

I manoeuvred the car gingerly out of the thorns, back onto the road. We climbed out to survey the situation. There was a deep ditch a few yards behind, and a few yards in front of us, on the left side of the road. Only in that spot, had there been a tiny space for us to swing off the road. Truly God Himself had rescued us. Also, had we been a few hundred yards further back, the approaching rally car would have been on the pebbly road and there would have been no cloud of dust to warn us.

We checked to see that there were no more clouds of dust approaching, held hands and thanked our Heavenly Father for his care. Then we went on our way, shaken but rejoicing.

The following Sunday, speaking at a morning service under a shady tree, I talked about the Safari of Life that we are all travelling in this world. God has, in his love, given us a good map to follow on our Safari – his Word, the Bible. Even more wonderful, he has given us a Navigator, Jesus our Saviour and Friend, to travel with us, to direct us and keep us on route. He gives us pit stops for rest and repairs, and a wonderful support team to cheer us on our way. Fellow travellers encourage us to keep on till the end of the race.

I challenged my listeners at the close of the service 'Have you invited your Navigator, Jesus, God's Son, to safari with you? Are you studying your route-map, the Bible, that will guide you, warn you of the dangers and the wrong turns along the journey? Are you obeying your loving Navigator as He travels the route with you? Set your eyes on the end of the journey, so that you win your race and receive your prize – the "Well Done" from the Captain of this great Safari - God.'

The listeners looked thoughtful as they drifted back to their homes at the end of the service. I prayed in my heart that all of us would 'run with patience the particular race that God has set before us, keeping our eyes on Jesus, our leader and instructor.' (Hebrews 12:1-2)

God bless you, reader. Happy safari!

Who is Lorna Eglin?

Lorna is an AIM missionary in South Africa. Her years in Kenya brought her into contact with many boys and girls from African tribes like the Maasai. Many of the young people she taught while on her own missionary safari in Kenya went on to hold positions of authority in the modern Kenya. One became the first Maasai lady doctor.

Other books by Lorna Eglin:

A Boy of Two Worlds ISBN 978-1-84550-126-6

A Girl of Two Worlds ISBN 978-1-85792-839-6

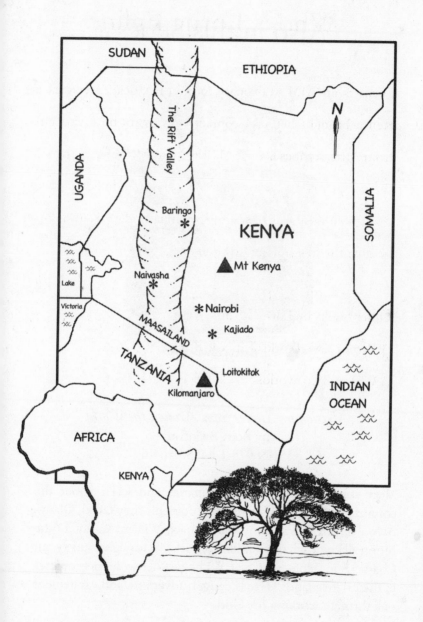

Also in this Series

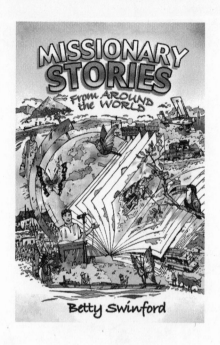

Missionary Stories from Around the World
by Betty Swinford
ISBN 978-1-84550-564-6

Meet some adventurous missionaries and learn about the countries they worked in and the problems they faced. Gladys Aylward, Jim Elliot, Amy Carmichael, William Carey, Lottie Moon all knew what it was like to work in a foreign country but Charles Spurgeon and Chief White Feather were missionaries in their native lands. Here is danger, adventure and excitement - all through working for God.

If you liked this book you'll love these

African Adventures

9781857928075

Cambodian Adventures

9781845504748

Wild West Adventures

9781845500658

Scottish Highland Adventures

9781845502812

Himalayan Adventures

9781845500801

AFRICAN Adventures

Dick Anderson

Cambodian Adventures

Donna Vann

HIMALAYAN Adventures

Penny Reeve

WILD WEST Adventures

Donna Vann

SCOTTISH HIGHLAND Adventures

Catherine Mackenzie

If you liked this book you'll love these

Jungle Doctor Spots a Leopard

9781845503017

Jungle Doctor Meets a Lion

9781845503925

Jungle Doctor on Safari

9781845503918

Jungle Doctor Pulls a Leg

9781845503895

Jungle Doctor's Africa

9781845503888

See all titles available in this series at

www.christianfocus.com

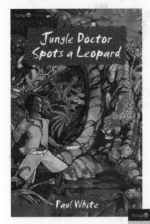

Jungle Doctor
Spots a Leopard

Paul White

Jungle Doctor
meets a lion

Paul White

Jungle Doctor's
Africa

Paul White

Jungle Doctor
on Safari

Paul White

Jungle Doctor
Pulls a Leg

Paul White

CHRISTIAN FOCUS PUBLICATIONS

Christian Focus   Christian Heritage   CF4K   Mentor

Christian Focus Publications publishes books for adults and children under its four main imprints: Christian Focus, Christian Heritage, CF4K and Mentor. Our books reflect that God's word is reliable and Jesus is the way to know him, and live for ever with him.

Our children's publication list includes a Sunday school curriculum that covers pre-school to early teens; puzzle and activity books. We also publish personal and family devotional titles, biographies and inspirational stories that children will love.

If you are looking for quality Bible teaching for children then we have an excellent range of Bible story and age specific theological books. From pre-school to teenage fiction, we have it covered!

**Find us at our web page:
www.christianfocus.com**

CF4·K
Because you're never
too young to know Jesus